Penguin Books

IS ANYONE THERE?

Is anyone there who understands me, cares about me, or has had the same problems that face me now? Can anyone help me to cope with losing my girlfriend/boyfriend, teach me how to make friends and live with other people? Is there anyone who understands how lonely I am, and why life suddenly isn't worth living?

Perhaps someone who picks up this book has been through one or all of these crises? Most of us have. Most of the time we come through them and look back and see them as just part of becoming an adult. But sometimes these experiences are something we can't handle and it's a comfort to find that other people have been there too!

This is what this book tries to do. It talks about some of the problems we all face or have faced and by the very telling puts them into some kind of perspective, relieving some of the misery the reader is suffering. It is undeniable that reading about an experience can often make it less traumatic when or if it happens.

So we offer you a collection of stories and articles, written by some of the finest writers today because they genuinely wanted to help, exploring, dissecting, explaining, and most of all *understanding* the problems that can face everyone.

+ *Plus* ▸

IS ANYONE THERE?

Edited by Monica Dickens
and Rosemary Sutcliff

Contents

Acknowledgements

The publishers and editors would like to thank the following for their kind permission to include their material in this book:

Joan Aiken for 'I Am Lonely', copyright © Joan Aiken, 1978; Lynne Reid Banks for 'The Aggie Match', copyright © Lynne Reid Banks, 1978; Roy Brown for 'Take-Off Point', copyright © Roy Brown, 1978; Roald Dahl and Michael Joseph Ltd for 'The Soldier', from *Someone Like You*, 1961, copyright © Roald Dahl, 1961; Margaret Forster for 'Teenage Depression', copyright © Margaret Forster, 1978; Jane Gardam for 'Transit Passengers', copyright © Jane Gardam, 1978; Leon Garfield for 'Bubblefoot', copyright © Leon Garfield, 1978; Alan Garner for 'The Edge of the Ceiling', copyright © Alan Garner, 1978; Ursula Le Guin and Victor Gollancz Ltd for an extract from *A Very Long Way from Anywhere Else*, 1976, copyright © Ursula Le Guin, 1976; Rosemary Harris for 'A World Out There for Me', copyright © Rosemary Harris, 1978; Susan Hill and Hamish Hamilton Ltd for 'The Badness Within Him', from *A Bit of Singing and Dancing*, 1973, copyright © Susan Hill, 1971; Jan Mark for 'I Was Adored Once Too', copyright © Jan Mark, 1978; Brian Patten and Allen & Unwin for 'Making a Call' from *Notes to the Hurrying Man*, 1969, copyright © Allen & Unwin, 1969, 'If You Had to Hazard a Guess, Who Would You Say Your Poetry Is For?' from *Vanishing Tricks*, 1976, copyright © Allen & Unwin, 1976, and 'Somewhere Between Heaven and Woolworth's' and 'In Numerous City Gardens' from *Little Johnny's Confession*, 1967, copyright © Allen & Unwin, 1967; Jeremy Seabrook for 'Teenage Suicide', copyright © Jeremy Seabrook, 1978; Robert Westall for 'Hetero, Homo, Bi or Nothing', copyright © Robert Westall, 1978. We have been unable to trace Angela Irene Stratton, who wrote 'Tommy', first published in *Children as Writers*, Daily Mirror, 1962, and reproduced by kind permission of the *Daily Mirror* Children's Literary Competition.

Introduction

I had a lonely childhood and growing-up time. My parents loved me and I loved them; but I could never talk to them about the problems and fears and aching hopes deep inside me that I had most need to talk about to someone. And there was no one else.

So when Anthony Lawton, my godson, had the idea for *Is Anyone There?* and asked me to help, in the first place by writing to the people who we hoped would contribute a story or poem or article, I had a very personal reason for gladness in being involved in the production of a book about or for people as lonely as I once was, or even much lonelier.

ROSEMARY SUTCLIFF

These stories are about loneliness in all its guises. They are also about the desperate need of one human being for another. If there were no such need, there would be no loneliness, even if people were physically alone. In many of the stories is heard the unspoken cry: 'Is anyone there?' This book is offered as a tribute and a benefit to the Samaritans, whose volunteers all over the world are ready twenty-four hours a day to answer the question, 'Is anyone there?' with a simple, 'Yes.'

MONICA DICKENS

Making a Call
BRIAN PATTEN

Alone in a red phone booth escaping down the wires from myself
but never quite reappearing at the other end
where the warm fires and company of women tease loneliness,
add new dimensions, marshlands, to sadness.
An address book containing
its various memories of nakedness
fills out dullness, gives some hope but click!
down goes another phone.
Someone's just going out to dinner,
someone's too busy making money,
someone's just about to shoot himself!
All over cities people standing alone in red phone booths,
making frantic connections –
experts in communication
relating back to their own reflections in misted-up windows.
Why not just wait outside?
Ask the first to leave, Did you make a connection? No?
Then let's open lines to ourselves –
we want direct lines without mouthpieces,
want to work out new systems,
safeguards against our isolated wanderings.
Morning – telephone number sleeps with telephone number –
the rest recently woken from party floors, benches, bed-sitters,
shiver in the corners of tubes, buses,
wander down the paths of gatecrashed houses
– so tender to each other we stink! –
I dreamt one night the whole world slept together in a red phone
      booth,
woke alone there. Laughed at my ridiculous situation.

I Was Adored Once Too

JAN MARK

Birkett is not noteworthy or even visible at school. In the annual Shakespeare play, he's not on stage. He's up in a rickety crow's nest in the flies, operating the lighting switchboard which can instantly turn night to noon to dusk, like a lonely god. Until lonely Julie, with a walk-on part, begins to spend every rehearsal up there with him, fascinated by the floats and battens, the rose and amber floods, the subtle dimmers. Fascinated also, incredibly, by old Birk, everyone's freak, no one's friend.

Typical of old Birk to realize too late that Sir Andrew Aguecheek's words are his: 'I was adored once too.'

This is probably the funniest story in the book, and probably the saddest.

MONICA DICKENS

*

'In the beginning Birkett created the heaven and the earth,' said Birkett. 'And the earth was without form, and void; and darkness was upon the face of the deep.'

'Geddonwithit, Birk,' shouted voices in the darkness, up on the stage and down in the auditorium. Someone fell over a chair.

Working blind, he clipped off a length of wire and threaded it into the fuse.

'And the Spirit of Birkett moved upon the face of the waters . . .' He snapped the fuse back into its socket and put his hand on the master switch. '. . . And Birkett said, Let there be light: and there was light.'

At once, all the lights: white light from the floats and the battens, rose pink lights and amber from the floods, and eight suns hanging in the void beyond the stage, four on each side of the hall.

'Not bad, not bad,' said Cosgrove, who was standing a few feet away and had heard everything that he said. 'Now let's see you make a man.'

Birkett leaned over the rail of his crow's-nest by the switchboard and looked round the edge of the curtain. Way below the white giants a red dwarf was approaching the footlights, surrounded by a nebula: Mr Anderson, head of English, with his everlasting fag and his chequered cheese-cutter pulled well down over his eyes to protect them from the glare.

What could they call him but Andy Capp? They called him Andy Capp.

Andy Capp came up to the edge of the stage and leaned across the floats, shielding himself from them by cupping his hands under his eyes and peering through the mask of black shadow like a seedy bandit.

'When Birkett has finished trying to blow his hand off, perhaps we can get on with the rehearsal?'

Birkett drew back from the edge of his cast-iron cradle and set his hands to the dimmer switches. His lighting plot was tacked up above them, secretively recorded in his own shorthand:

P36 l.15 exit M. D_1 down 5 D_2 down 10 simul.

l.20 D_2 down 0 $D_3/4$ down 5 change spots to dim *here* 1/2/3/4/.

The light came and went at his command. He was far less likely to blow off his hand than was Andy Capp himself. When Andy Capp came up on stage and stood at the foot of Birkett's vertical iron ladder, Birkett wanted nothing so much as to put his boot on Andy Capp's head and screw it down into the floor, as the English teacher screwed down his own boot on his fag ends.

Andy Capp knew this as well as Birkett did, and stayed on the other side of the footlights, within spitting distance of Birkett but safe; because Andy Capp was Sir and Birkett was in 5b, good for fiddling with the lights and little else.

Fiddling was the right word. Birkett played on his dimmers with the love and skill of a virtuoso violinist, making night and day, the greater light and the lesser, with the tenderest touch of his long and flexible fingers. The woodwork master, now Stage Manager, was well aware of this, which was why he had given Birkett the lighting plot instead of doing it himself. As far as Andy Capp was concerned, Birkett was marooned on top of his ladder because he could do less damage there than he could on stage, mangling Shakespeare.

And he could mend a fuse in the dark.

Birkett consulted the plot and, without looking, placed his unerring hands on the dimmers. His eye was on the stage where Cosgrove, a pillow stuffed under his sweater, was reeling from side to side, supposedly drunk. Cosgrove, when genuinely drunk, was nothing like this, but after the effects had worn off he never could remember what it *had* been like. Cosgrove's mates had sworn to have him tanked up on the night so as to get an authentic performance out of him.

'Listen, Cosgrove,' said Andy Capp. Birkett's hands froze on the dimmers. 'This is *Twelfth Night*, not Saturday night at the Bricklayer's Arms. Sir Toby Belch is supposed to be tipsy in this scene, not paralytic.'

Cosgrove snapped upright and Howell, who was playing Sir Andrew Aguecheek, was knocked flying by the cushion. He went spinning across the stage, stiff-legged, like dividers across a map.

'Aguecheek,' said Andy Capp, 'is a foolish knight, not a berserk ballerina. Keep your twinkle toes on the ground. Get on with it, rabble.' His eyes slid upwards and sideways. Birkett knew that Andy Capp had something offensive ready to say to him as well, but there was no occasion to say it. Sir Toby and Sir Andrew faced each other; Sir Andrew's mouth opened and the dimmers began to move.

'Before me, she's a good wench,' said Sir Andrew.

'She's a beagle, true-bred, and one that adores me; what o' that?'

Sir Andrew raised his eyebrows. 'I was adored once, too.'

'Howell! Don't sound so bloody chatty,' Andy Capp bellowed from the darkness. 'That's one of your better lines. Make something of it. Like this.' He minced about beyond the footlights, now in focus, now out. 'I was adored once *too*.'

'Oh, ducky,' murmured Cosgrove, out of the corner of his mouth.

'Get a laugh there,' said Andy Capp. 'It's the last one you'll get in this scene. And Birkett, keep your hot little hands off those dimmers. Are you trying to black us out?' Birkett let his hands drop. He had planned to make the light turn cold on that line, dimming out the amber and the rose, leaving only the white and blue battens. He had not bargained for a laugh; it didn't strike him as funny. There was a character in the play known as the Clown, but he was a wise guy, a professional fool. Aguecheek was the real fool.

'I was adored once *too*,' said Howell, flimsy-wristed, gyrating on pleated ankles. He had tucked his trousers into his socks to make himself feel Elizabethan. There was an immediate laugh from the resting actors, out of sight in the dark hall.

'Again!' cried Andy Capp.

'I was adored once *too*.'

There were two more scenes before the end of the act. On the stage below the players strutted, and at the switchboard above Birkett lightened their darkness and darkened their days. He felt as remote as God, operating the firmament; whatever was going on down there had nothing to do with him. The pain and the pleasure were outside his influence and he felt them only in terms of the coloured filters required to light each scene: blue and green for sorrow, pink and gold for joy, so that when he looked at the brilliant aquarium that was the stage he saw chaos. People hid behind hedges, assumed false names, slipped into disguises and climbed out of them. Lesley Pascoe, smooth and slender, golden girl of the High School, was cast as Viola, identical twin to Sebastian, and Sebastian was played by swarthy Noddy Newton who was so covered with thick black hair that when he tried on his costume it sprouted through the legs of his tights like winter wheat after a wet autumn.

All the female roles were being played by girls borrowed from the High School. As well as the three principals a number of friends turned up at each rehearsal to understudy or provide moral support in case anyone got jumped on in a dark cloakroom. Birkett knew none of them. They were the girls who went round with the boys who were down there on the stage; none of them people who would go round with Birkett.

It was nothing to do with him. He saw it and heard it and was out of it; even so, the words stayed in his mind, like dust caught in a net curtain. In the same way, and without wanting to, he had memorized the Bible. For years he had been a regular worshipper, with his parents, at the green tin chapel behind the bus station. One Sunday he had suddenly realized that he was no longer worshipping and after a month or two he stopped going there, but the damage was done already. It was widely believed that Birkett had sold his soul to the chapel and was stricken unable to enjoy himself, drink beer or think about women. People half expected him to turn up on the doorstep with leaflets, at inconvenient moments.

He looked down from the switchboard, one of them, but not one with them.

'To the gates of Tartar, thou most excellent devil of wit!' Sir Toby shouted. He strode off stage and made a mock run up the ladder, repelled suddenly by the impact of his cushion against the rungs.

'And I'll make one too,' said Sir Andrew Aguecheek, with total irrelevance, as it seemed to Birkett. He wandered off in the other direction.

Cosgrove's spotty brother, who was prompter and Assistant Stage Manager, swung on the knotted rope that dangled beside his chair. The curtains closed on Birkett's sunlit stage and Act Two was over. Cosgrove poked the cushion out of his sweater and looked up at Birkett.

'Don't you get struck by lightning for blasphemy?'

'Blasphemy?'

'Smitten with a plague of frogs?'

'Blasphemy?'

'Taking credit for the Universe,' said Cosgrove, but because Birkett had nothing laughable to say he lost interest and slid between the curtains, sylph-slim without his stomach which he left on-stage. He disappeared into the dark hall, followed by Howell.

'House lights!' Andy Capp was bawling. 'House lights, Birkett wake up for God's sake Birkett wake up Birkett . . .'

Howell put his head between the curtains again. 'Fiat lux, laddie. Fiat lux.' Howell knew Latin. Birkett didn't. The house lights were not his concern anyway; the switches were at the back of the hall, next to the wall bars. Finally someone remembered this and the lights were put on. Andy Capp's monotonous yelling subsided and cheerful conversation swelled up to fill the gap where it had been. Cups rattled. The girls who were not on stage had made themselves responsible for serving drinks (although no one had dared ask them to) which they prepared in the Sixth Form Common Room and brought to the hall on trays. The spotty brother and other backstage personnel went through the curtains for coffee and fodder. Birkett stayed at the switchboard, setting up his lights for the next act. It was the same scene, but a different time of day:

Olivia's Garden. Full battens white 1/2 dim 0 blue 3. Amber floods full floats. 1/2/3/4/ spots up full 5/6 down 8.

He made morning.

Number 6 dimmer was grating in its runner. Knowing that he had a quarter of an hour before Andy Capp drove the cast back to work Birkett took out a screwdriver and began to remove the casing. He first put up the master switch and worked in darkness, only his careful hands illuminated by the meagre glow from a badly shuttered window in the changing room behind him. In the corner of his eye he saw a narrow light spread across the stage and ebb again as someone opened the curtains and slipped through. Finished with the dimmer he replaced the casing and threw the master switch. There came an angry squeak from the foot of the ladder.

'Ow. Now you've made me spill it.'

One of the girls was standing there, clasping a thick china cup of slopped coffee. Birkett leaned over the rail.

'Was that my fault?'

'You made me jump, putting all the lights on like that.' She squinted up at him. He looked at the coffee cup.

'You haven't lost much. There's plenty left.'

'It isn't mine.'

'There's no one else here,' said Birkett.

'You're here.'

'Is it for me?' Nobody had brought him coffee before. There was no reason why he should not join the others in the hall, but apart from wanting a drink there was no reason why he should. He preferred to do without the drink.

'I suppose it must be,' she said. 'I was handing it out and Tony Cosgrove said "Don't forget God, back there," so I brought it through. Do they call you God?'

'They call me Birk,' said Birkett.

'Well, do you want the coffee or don't you, Birk?' said the girl. 'I'm not going to call you that,' she said crossly. 'What's your real name?'

'Reuben,' said Birkett, reluctantly. The Twelve Tribes of Israel were highly thought of at the tin chapel. He disliked admitting to Reuben, but he had no second name. It could have been worse. It could have been Zebulun. Or Gad.

'I'm Juliet.' She offered him the coffee, but when he made no move to take it she withdrew her hand. 'Call me Julie. Can I come up?'

'Juliet will do.' It didn't occur to him that one could suffer as much from Juliet as from Reuben. 'You can come up if you like.'

She stood on tiptoe and placed the cup on the floor of the cradle. It was difficult for her to stand more on tiptoe than she did already: her wedge heels were very high.

'You'd better take your shoes off,' he advised. She looked suspicious, as if he had made an improper suggestion and her friends had warned her about people like him, but she came up the ladder, her lumpy heels going glamp glamp glamp as they struck the iron rungs.

'You are a bit like God, so high up,' she said, leaning against the rail. Birkett, pressed for space, had to turn round with extreme care in case she thought he was making advances.

'Turn the lights off again,' she said.

Now who's making advances? he wondered, as the darkness crashed down.

'It's snug up here.'

'About as snug as an oil rig.' Now that it was entirely dark he was aware of the draught from the changing-room window and the smell of old lunches that never quite died because the stage had once been used as a canteen, before the new one was built. The hot lights seemed to revive them. He pulled the switch again and Juliet stood blinking beside him.

'Birkett, stop b-ing about with those lights,' shouted Andy Capp, mindful that there were ladies present.

'Aren't you going to drink your coffee?' said Juliet. Birkett stepped forward to pick up the cup and managed to kick it over the edge of the cradle. It didn't break, but a greyer stain spread over the grey stage cloth.

'I'm always doing things like that,' he said.

'I was beginning to think you never did anything,' said Juliet, and went glamping down the ladder again. He put his head under the lower rail and watched her go.

'Are you in the play?' he said. 'I've never seen you on stage.'

'I'm a servant. Page sixty, Act Three, Scene Four, don't blink or you'll miss me.' He didn't say that he thought she was wasted as a servant. 'I'm understudying Maria, too.'

'That's the maid, isn't it?'

'It's the best part,' she said, quickly.

'I thought Lesley Pascoe . . .'

'Oh, Viola. That's nothing much. Maria's got the best lines of all the women. And she's funny,' said Juliet. She went towards the curtains with the empty cup. 'It's the best part . . . but you wouldn't know,' she said, and vanished.

She was right. He didn't know.

That night he read the play right through for the first time, and he was surprised to discover how much of it he knew already. He agreed that Maria was the best of the women's parts, but he doubted that Juliet would make much of a showing in it. Maria was a stinger; little, quick-witted, malicious. He thought of Juliet's large hopeful face and pile-driver legs.

On Thursday evening, when they stopped for a break, there was Juliet coming up the ladder glamp glamp glamp with two cups of coffee and a Kit-Kat. His half of the Kit-Kat played merry hell with his demon back tooth, but he suffered in silence, showing her how the dimmers worked and explaining the runic mysteries of his lighting plot.

'Do you manage all this by yourself? I wouldn't have thought you'd have enough hands.'

He spread his fingers across the board and moved all eight dimmers at once.

'Like a pianist,' Juliet said. 'Stretching octaves. What about if you need to turn something else on, at the same time?'

'I use my nose. No, I *do*. In the mad scene where Malvolio thinks he's in the nut-house: I turn off this switch here with my nose. Like this.'

'Well, it's long enough.' Juliet didn't seem to think that it was a very nice accomplishment. 'You need Tony Cosgrove up here. He's all hands.'

'He'd be no good,' said Birkett. 'He'd be talking all the time. You have to pay attention.'

'There's no one to talk to.'

'There would be if Cosgrove was here.'

At the end of the break Juliet remained at the top of the ladder.

'You don't mind if I stay?'

'Of course not.' He should have said, Oh please, do. In fact, he did mind. The cradle was built to take at most two people, both working. There was no room for ballast. Birkett was used to availing himself of the whole area and the need to tread carefully spoiled his concentration. For the first time he missed a lighting cue and was rewarded by a blast of scorching scorn from Andy Capp, who happened to notice, for once. The sympathetic touch of Juliet's hand on his arm was no reward, and no consolation, either.

Cosgrove, bleary and becushioned, leered at him, one finger laid to the side of his nose.

'Nudge nudge, wink wink,' said Cosgrove, when he came off stage at the end of the scene and Birkett was embarrassed in the dark; but at the same time mildly gratified that Cosgrove imagined him to be having his evil way – as Cosgrove certainly would have been, in his place.

At the next rehearsal Juliet was up there before him.

'Aren't you on in this scene?'

'Fancy you noticing.'

'I read the play.' He had read it again since last week. He was beginning to admire the way it was put together; two quite different stories spliced like cords, ending in a neat knot, but he didn't find it very funny and parts of it struck him as miserably cruel. He had always regarded Shakespeare as an effete twit who couldn't write a straight sentence to save his life, but he was beginning to see that Shakespeare might have got along very well with Andy Capp.

'Another bride, another groom, another sunny hu-hunny-moon,' sang Cosgrove at the foot of the ladder. 'Make with the sunshine, Birk.'

Juliet was picking her way through the lighting plot.

'I don't expect anyone but us understands this,' she said happily, building an intimate secret where there was neither secret nor intimacy. 'I'm not on stage until here, look. I can run round the back, just before.'

And she did: and as soon as her little part was done she ran back again. Birkett did not hear her coming up the ladder. She had taken her shoes off.

'Don't you want to go for coffee?' said Birkett, when the break came.

'I asked Lesley to bring us some.' He guessed why she had asked Lesley when Lesley came through the curtains with a sulky shove, carrying a cup in either hand.

'Too busy to fetch your own?'

Juliet smiled a little, and then laughed, because the light was too dim for the smile to show. Birkett waited until Lesley had gone before sitting down to drink his coffee.

'It's a good thing we aren't fat,' said Juliet.

'Eh?'

'There's not much room up here.'

'We could always sit on the stage.' He stood up to consult the plot.

'Hey, Roo.' He supposed that it was short for Reuben.

'Yes?'

'I'm glad I'm not Viola.'

'You're even less like Noddy than Lesley is.'

'That's not what I meant. She's on stage, all through the play.'

'Not all the time.'

'No, but on-off-on-off. It's the same with Maria. Suzanne's playing Maria. Do you know Suzanne? She's all sweaty by the end of the evening, from rushing about.'

'Dodging Cosgrove?'

'And that. I used to wish she'd be ill for a bit so that I'd get a chance at Maria; tonsillitis or something. She's got terrible tonsils, all her family have. When she turns her head you can see great lumps in her neck – just here.' She put her cool hand on his throat.

'I've had mine out,' said Birkett.

'I don't wish that any more.'

'Wish what?'

'That Suzanne would get tonsillitis. I'd sooner be here than on stage.'

'Well, I wouldn't wish anyone had tonsillitis,' said Birkett. 'Except Andy Capp, maybe. It might shut him up.'

'Roo, why do you call him Andy Capp?'

'Oh God, look at him,' said Birkett. 'All he needs is a pigeon on his head.'

'What's his wife like? Florrie?'

'More like the Statue of Liberty. No, really. He hardly comes up to her chin.'

'Have they got any children?'

'Three.'

'I like children,' said Juliet. 'I'd like a lot of children.'

There was only one week left before opening night. In front of the curtain the stage had been extended by building it up with prefabricated blocks. Andy Capp called it the apron.

When the third act ended, Howell climbed over the apron and came through the curtains with the coffee. Juliet arranged for it to be delivered by a different person each time, and Birkett no longer wondered why.

'Working overtime, Birk?' said Howell. He stood on the bottom rung of the ladder and rested his chin on the top, level with their feet.

'Push off, Face-ache,' said Birkett.

'Aguecheek – Agueface – Face-ache; good thinking, Batman,' said Howell, sinking from sight. He reappeared a moment later, meandering across the stage in his Aguecheek walk, knees together, toes apart.

'You missed your cue again, in Scene Four,' said Howell. 'Do you know what Andy Capp said? "Bloody Birkett, busy with his skirt." '

'He never said that.' Beside him Juliet gave a little gasp, intending to sound outraged; only sounding pleased.

'It was said though,' said Howell. 'Your Birk-type secret is out, Birk.' He sprang backwards between the curtains. Nemesis got him. Someone had removed the block in the middle of the apron, and Birkett heard the crunch as he hit the floor.

'He's broken his leg; in two places. Should have been his neck,' said Andy Capp. 'He's in traction. Silly b.' There were ladies present.

'What about my bruvver?' said Cosgrove. 'He's been prompter ever since we started. He knows the whole thing right through.'

'He couldn't play Aguecheek.'

'He could probably play Viola if you twisted his arm.'

'God forbid,' said Andy Capp. 'Anyway, we're not having him on stage. Remember the carol concert?'

'Someone else knows it by heart,' said Cosgrove. He silently indicated the switchboard with his thumb. 'He remembers everything. He knows half the Bible for a start.'

'Birkett? He can't put one foot in front of the other without falling over.'

'Who'd notice? He's a dead ringer for Aguecheek,' said Cosgrove. 'You wouldn't even have to make him up.'

'Birkett! Get down here,' Andy Capp shouted. 'If you can spare the time,' he added, for the benefit of the cast. Birkett climbed down the ladder and approached the group in the middle of the stage.

'Good of you to drop in,' said Andy Capp. 'I'm sure you've got more interesting things to do. Cosgrove here says you're a quick study.'

'A what?'

'A quick study, har har,' said Andy Capp. 'He says you learn things easily.'

'Not me,' said Birkett.

'He thinks you know the whole play.'

'Not me.'

'Come off it,' said Cosgrove. 'You've been sitting up there watching us for the past six months. You must know it.'

Birkett guessed what they were after.

'Not me.'

'Not I,' said Andy Capp.

Cosgrove put on his cushion and his Sir Toby voice and said sharply, 'Did she see thee the while, old boy? tell me that.'

'As plain as I see you now,' said Birkett, without thinking.

'Art thou good at these kick-shaws, knight?'

'As any man in Illyria, whatsoever he be, under the degree of my betters; and yet I will not compare with an old man,' said Birkett.

'She's a beagle, true-bred, and one that adores me; what o' that?'

'I was adored once too.'

'Beat that,' said Cosgrove.

Andy Capp thrust a book into Birkett's hands. 'There you are, Aguecheek. Get on with it.'

'But I don't understand it all.'

'Then you'll have a lot in common with the audience,' said Andy Capp. 'You have a week. Get on with it.'

'Who'll do the lights?' said Birkett. 'I'm the only one who knows the plot.'

'Damn the lights. What's the good of lights if we have no play?' said Andy Capp. 'Leave 'em all switched on. Come on, rabble. Act One, Scene Three.'

The rehearsal got under way. Birkett held the book in his hands and never looked at it once. When it was his turn to speak he spoke, helplessly, the very words that Howell had spoken, and in the very tone that Howell had spoken them.

'Proper polly parrot, aren't you?' muttered Cosgrove, when he stumbled on his lines and Birkett prompted him, still without looking at the book. 'You taking English A level, next year?'

'You're joking.'

'Do it. You'll have a walk-over.'

At the end of the scene Birkett ran from the stage and made for the ladder, hoping that he would have time to get up there and adjust the lights before he was wanted, but as he put his hands to the rungs the floods came on and the dimmers went up. Juliet looked over the railing.

'Don't worry about me, Roo. I can manage.'

He hadn't been worrying about her. He had forgotten that she was there.

'I told you I could understand it.'

'Better leave it,' said Birkett, furious at finding his true place usurped. 'I've made alterations – you won't be able to follow them.'

'I know your writing,' said Juliet, comfortably. 'Go back on stage. You're doing ever so well. I didn't know you were so good.'

'I'm not,' he growled, and thought it was true. He was a proper polly parrot.

'You, Birkett, are a double-dyed creep,' said Andy Capp, leaning across the apron. 'Is this the case that dropped a thousand bricks? Is this the celebrated numb-skull who has forgotten to hand in his homework six weeks out of nine? Well, we've found you out now, you twister.'

'Polly parrot,' said Birkett, under his breath.

'Get on with it, rabble.'

They got on with it, and Juliet got on with the lights. Birkett knew to the second when a change was due, and to the second the changes were made. He made a note to dim Number Two spot when he had the chance. It shone straight in his eye every time he faced right.

'Excellent,' Sir Toby roared in his ear. 'I smell a device.'

'I have't in my nose too,' said Birkett, in a reedy nasal whine, out-Howelling Howell. A happy laugh surged out of the darkness.

Sir Toby roared longer and louder, piqued that Birkett was getting bigger laughs than he was.

'My purpose is indeed a horse of that colour,' said Maria, arching her long neck like a thoroughbred. Birkett could see no sign of swollen tonsils.

'And your horse would now make him an ass,' he said, and was half drowned by another high tide of laughter. They were laughing at him, not with him, but he supposed that that was what he was there for.

Maria spoke again and went out, blowing coy kisses to Sir Toby.

'Goodnight, Penthesilia,' said Sir Toby.

'Before me, she's a good wench,' said Birkett.

'She's a beagle, true-bred, and one that adores me; what o' that?'

'I was adored once too.' The laughter exploded all round him as he stood there, a dead ringer for Sir Andrew Aguecheek; lank yellow hair hanging over his white face, round eyes staring, long arms dangling. What a thought; Birkett; adored; har har, as Andy Capp would say.

Suddenly the lights turned blue, stuttered, went dim, became bright again, went out entirely and then came on in a frightful blaze, all eight suns burning him alive.

'What the hell is going on?' demanded Andy Capp, vaulting on to the apron like a galvanized leprechaun and hurling his copy of the play across the stage. 'Who did that?'

Birkett turned to the switchboard in a rage.

'You silly cow! Leave it alone. I altered that bit. I said you wouldn't understand it.'

'Who's up there? Who is it? Come down here, now,' said Andy Capp, more terrible in a whisper than he ever was at full volume.

Juliet came down the ladder glamp glamp glamp on her club heels and stumbled towards them. Her face was a brighter pink than any floodlight could have made it, and her eyes were enormous with tears.

'I thought . . .'

'Thought?' Andy Capp was incredulous. 'Who asked you to think? Who asked you to touch the switchboard? It's a skilled job, not a game for silly little girls.'

Juliet moved towards Birkett. Birkett moved away.

'I told you,' he said.

'I thought I knew it,' said Juliet. She bent her head and the tears fell to the floor. They made greyer spots on the grey stage cloth. 'I thought I had it right. I'm always up there.'

'Don't we know it? And we know why: you made sure of that,' said Andy Capp, unforgivably. 'Now get off the stage and get out of the way, there's a good girl. Do your courting out of school, next time.'

Juliet tried to look at Birkett. Birkett looked up at the proscenium arch. The second amber flood was dead. He thought there might be a spare bulb in the box below the switchboard.

If not, he would have to get one ordered tomorrow. When he looked round again, Juliet was gone, climbing awkwardly over the apron and down into the hall. The darkness took her. Andy Capp followed.

'Get on with it, rabble.'

'Goodnight, Penthesilia,' said Sir Toby.

'Before me, she's a good wench.'

'She's a beagle, true-bred, and one that adores me; what o' that?'

'I was adored once too,' said Birkett.

A World Out There for Me
ROSEMARY HARRIS

Pete Townshend, leader of the rock group 'The Who', comes across as very honest, very likeable in this interview. Expectably, he talks about the pitfalls of success. All the nicest stars allow us that sweet consolation of knowing it's not all roses at the top. Unexpectedly, after giving us his simple key for coping with trouble – accepting things *as they are* – he adds disarmingly '... other times, of course, my moods prevent me from doing it. I say, well, that might work, but I'm not bloody well going to do it, so there.'

Thousands of people wrote to him about his music: 'Yes, that's me!' and this interview is going to have the same effect. He has all the star qualities – more talent, energy, drive, charm than the rest of us – but has also experienced all our depressions, guilts and insecurities. Before he was seventeen he used to catch himself envying people who sat back and said, 'I could have made it, if only I'd had a break.' The magic 'if' absolved them handily from trying. For Pete Townshend, there never were any 'ifs'. He created his own breaks. After you read this, you may understand how, and go back peacefully to, 'If only ...'

MONICA DICKENS

*

Where Thoreau wrote 'The mass of men lead lives of quiet desperation' it's easy to imagine he was writing of the mental climate in England today rather than America of the last century. When so many older faces wear expressions of gloomy frustration, it's not surprising that so many younger people and adolescents seem bogged down with massive desperation, nor that the extremists take to tangling with the police, while the gentler sort sit at home, holding their heads in their hands, and refusing invitations to come out and have a nice cuppa tea. But putting aside the strains of real illness, or grief, can anything positive be said about depression which won't sound like telling the sufferer to 'pull yourself together' – as if the whole being had developed a suet-pudding collapse that could have been prevented by a piece of elastic round the waist?

Sometimes, at least, a deal of creativity can be milked from depression and allied states, if the energy patterns can be changed. Brooding on this question of despair and creativity, I went to talk to Pete Townshend, leader of the rock group 'The Who', whose spectacular energy and equally spectacular success with 'Tommy' have been such landmarks of his generation. I went, not just because Pete has become something of a cult figure in this country and the outer world, but because I'd heard him speak at times of his own past sense of isolation, and sporadic despairs. It's hard to describe him, because if you like somebody the word often used is 'nice', an expression I hate.

As we're both rather long-nosed and were both looking faintly anxious, I thought we probably looked like two borzois worrying a bone. We sat in the quiet room overlooking the river, in the house that Pete has built at Twickenham and dedicated to Meher Baba. Pete turned on the tape recorder and we began to talk.

R: You've felt a good deal of despair and isolation at one time or another, Pete, and I was wondering if you'd tell me if there was any way that you managed to get through the outer circumstances, or the inner – broke through to yourself, or to the outer world?

PETE: I don't know whether any experiences that I've had are really unique, but I have experienced through work, particularly when very young – and sometimes through drugs – a pretty desperate state; probably something I'd share with lots of other young people. The deepest, explosive things that happened to me have really been when I felt that I transgressed some unwritten law that I carry around in my heart; when I do something that I've enjoyed tremendously, but felt in some way that I've betrayed myself.

It's the feeling of hypocrisy I can't stand living with – and because you can't undo the past, you just have to live with it. So for me Meher Baba is not only a very important person, because his philosophies happen to suit me, and I happen to like the way he lived his life, and the people he produced, but because basically I do need somebody that I can believe is a *touchable* God – reachable, believable.

I have to be able to feel that I can say to somebody: 'Listen, this is what I did: I was on tour, got drunk, smashed up a room, somebody got hurt – and then I engaged in a sexual encounter with three men and a dog!' Or something – whatever happens to be bugging me at the time.

I've never had any *real* problems with drugs – in the last eight or nine years, they've not interested me. But drink and sex, hand in hand, in my business, are two things very difficult to keep away from. I think every individual has a standard which he has to live by. And I found that my mouth was saying things, publicly – that I was writing things directly to young people through my music; and young people would write to me and say 'You've changed my life, given me hope ...' And on the other hand I was living another kind of life, indulgent, impetuous – and that led to fantastic depressions where on occasions I felt that even Baba couldn't help me.

R: What about, say, the age of fifteen? As an adult, you've got your sustaining belief in Baba – you've got things going for you in your work. But what about that earlier stage when people are in family situations, school situations, where they may feel totally isolated, but full of sexual and other energies going into depression?

PETE: I had a pretty typical adolescence; a – er – little bit of a dodgy, uncertain childhood. But by the time I was about twelve my parents had another son, and then another – that consolidated the family very much, and I felt very secure. The interesting thing is, I suppose, that going through all the normal things: feeling like the smallest guy in the gang, the one that got picked on, made the most fun of, most unattractive child, etc. – I've got piles of letters from people, with all that, could reach to the ceiling! The whole *population* feels like that! Either like that – or they're so stuck up that they're unapproachable.

Well, I've been playing guitar since I was about twelve, y'see. Right through my very difficult period. Now, 1977 passed with the emergence of easily put together simple groups of kids calling themselves Punk groups – just people able to play. It's a great form of expression. It's like a guy came to see me yesterday from a group – an' told me they had a singer just joined them while Punk music was aggressive – and since it's started to soften up a bit has gone back to mugging: literally! He was muggin' people, then went to sing with the group, and now he's back to muggin'. But the other boys in the group are still playing – obviously, for them, it's not violence of expression that's important, but the fact that musical expression allows them something more complete, more fulfilling.

When I was faced with a problem that I felt I couldn't handle (here Pete listed them with retrospective relish, from first jiving and hang-ups with girls, to robbery and violence) I just used to run back to my guitar . . . and in the end this guitar became a symbol, the thing I realized all my energy was going into. I played an' played an' played – and as such it became a release valve.

R: When people talk about isolation, what they often mean is that they've found nothing in themselves with which they can bridge the gap – as your guitar did for you. What would you say to them?

PETE: You don't have to be depressed to feel isolated or alone – You can feel quite precious about it, until suddenly you do realize, maybe with a tremendous shock, that you've missed a helluva lot: perhaps through going to a party, and up to that point all parties have been awful, boring, everybody's been drunk, and suddenly you go to a party which is really wonderful – You sit and talk; you meet some women that you feel are human beings, you meet a couple of blokes that you respect; and suddenly you think: oh, no – it *is* possible – it's possible that I can find people that I'*m* like – You know, there is a world out there for me, and I've been avoiding actually facing up to that.

And that's a terrible blow. I think it hit me when I was about twenty-one, twenty-two, when I went to ask Karen to go out with me. It was my absolute certainty that she was going to tell me to bugger off – and then actually gettin' accepted! The Group was already quite famous, but we'd all tremendous jealousies because, say, Roger in the Group, the singer, was an attractive person, got his own way in that respect; Keith, the drummer of the Group, was very popular, very funny, extremely pretty, found getting girlfriends easy. John – our bass player – was secure, already engaged.

I just shut myself up in a Belgravia flat, an' churned out such things as 'My Generation'. They weren't FU's to Society, they were FU's to *everybody*. They were *my* cynical things. So, to realize there was somebody out there who didn't know me well, but was willing to take me at face value, was both a pleasant thing, and an amazing shock! Isolation or loneliness is something – people feel it in different ways. The stories that I hear – If I write a song about something I hear, or suffering that I see – Immediately I'd get the feed-back. People would show up here, at concerts, they'd fight their way, talk to me, might write me a letter – and of course that's the direct line. Because they open up – they open right up, and they say: 'Till I realized that you – that someone – felt like I did –' It's important for them to know someone does know what it's like.

The album I wrote called 'Quadrophenia' was nothing but the story of a young working-class mod kid, his inability to get on at home, at school, with a job, with girls – the only thing he had was his scooter – and he smashed that up; and then he made a suicide attempt which went wrong. It was an exercise in trying to portray what leads up to that thing that Meher Baba calls spiritual desperation. *He* says an aspirant on the spiritual path *has* to have experienced spiritual desperation; and of course it's every other kind of desperation rolled up; physical, mental, the whole thing. And so it was to point out that I felt that spiritual, or life desperation, might be ostensibly a bad thing, an awful thing, but it does, inevitably, lead to an opening of the heart, and in that respect it's a good thing.

R: Jung said that the dark shadow in man is ninety per cent pure gold. I think, in a sense, you've got to go *into* depression, can't just ignore it and pretend on the surface, superficially. It can be positive, but again, it's such a desperate state that unless you've a lifeline to outside, there's the danger of suiciding taking place, isn't there?

PETE: I've never actually – tried to commit suicide, or wanted to ... always had a way of reaching out and getting some support or some – attack. A response. I was talking to my mother-in-law (who's a Samaritan) an' saying that it's for this reason I would find it very difficult to be a Samaritan. For me it's so easy to find a – a *trick* to snap myself out of it. Like, for example, even doing something really explosive – I mean, not necessarily physically – which intimidates or re-establishes the strength of your own position to some extent. Maybe in that way I'm archetypal of my contemporaries, an' a lot of younger people who actually do lean on violence all the time to find their feet.

R: You always give me the feeling of someone who's relaxed

in his dealings with other people. But with some people you feel there's an *egg* of 'keep away' – or 'my parents said I should be neat and tidy'. Did your parents mould you into their way – or did they let you be yourself?

PETE: They let me be myself. My Dad was a musician – an' my mother started off life as a musician; very vitriolic and explosive people, both very open, equally likely to row as to express that they love one another. The only slight neurosis I developed was the fact that my mother's a lover of beautiful people – she was very beautiful in her own youth. I think she was kind of cheesed-off that she'd produced such a sort of plain son, and used to make that very clear. If she was angry with me, she used to come out with remarks . . . You know, I used to draw a parallel between them and the kind of things that kids at school would say. That did develop a slight *bitter* neurosis, a feeling that, right: I'll-show-the-lot-of-you, which tempered my – musical humility! I was quite prepared to go and join a band and strum away, not necessarily end up doing what I did, but it really was what hardened me up, and said, 'Right: I'm goin' to be *enormous*; I'm goin' to make millions of pounds, goin' to poke out at you from all the front pages'; and had I not enjoyed that particular experience . . .!

R: You reacted positively – A lot of people who need to feel that way would just go into a shell.

PETE: I didn't get that much of it, you see; the other thing was that I was allowed to leave home early on – when I was sixteen – and I think that was incredibly important. To discover Art School where there were intelligent women, new values, different music – and you're away from the soppy grammar school boy mentality and into something more real.

R: What about grammar school – were you pressurized to be like every other boy? If you weren't, was it something you were made to feel bad about?

PETE: It's hard for me to pinpoint exactly what was going on at school, now. A lot of the people I used to be around were

older than me, more mature, treated me, you know, with
affection – and I was literally smaller in those days, about five
foot six. Suddenly sprouted when I was eighteen – practically
a foot. Unbelievable to me and everybody else.

R: You weren't physically bullied, or anything? This can be
hell at school.

PETE: Not constantly! Occasiona'ly. I used to like associating
with villains . . . used to suffer from them to a great extent.
[Retrospective pleasure.] You know, I used to like being on
the fringes of villainy. Treacherously disloyal at the moment
of truth. Terrible lessons about the English police! If you give
us the name of your friend we'll let you off, and things like
that . . .

R: That side in oneself that wants to side with authority.

PETE: I hardened up. I never got properly chucked out of
school – I was a little bit mischievous, but not big enough to
cause that much trouble. We did have an extremely good
form master. Very very loved and respected bloke. By even
the hard nuts. A great man. But some subjects I was
interested in, I got lost because another teacher kept making
me a test case – and this used to annoy me. When you're
thirteen or fourteen, you've got this feeling that you're a
complete, total person; of your own rights to freedom, to
being an individual. You've got this escape clause written
into your heart which is really what makes you want to stay
alive: that if it really comes to the crunch, you can do what
you feel is right. And the worst thing about school is – when
you feel that perhaps it's authority that's trying to take it
away from you; trying to crush it.

R: Yes – it's this sense of living that's important, which you
start with; and if somebody's managed to take that away it
really leads to depression, to being substitute people – more
and more cut off – not real from the centre. And I think a lot
of people get very suicidal because they've never found a way
to that bit of themselves again that was taken away in child-

hood. But you give this impression of being a tremendously vital person who, whatever happened, his lifeline would always kind of wriggle him out of it somewhere!

PETE: Perhaps the thing is – when you realize that in a way you've got a choice ... There's a point in life – sometimes happens very early – when you've a choice to either make it or break it – It *almost* depends on what *mood* you're in. If you happen to be in the right mood when you're faced with the question, you go the right way; and if you're in the wrong mood –! I get very angry with my moods, because I don't necessarily identify with them entirely.

R: Is there something you find hard to cope with? I get terrible anger at moments when I should be cool –

PETE: I'm afraid I'm a believer in it! Like, it's one of the hardest things that I find to deal with – I remember one young guy coming to me and saying, 'This thing about Meher Baba saying you should suppress lust, greed and anger – But surely lust's a natural expression of attraction to another human being; why should you suppress it?' And I took this question to a higher authority, I think it was to Murshida, and she wrote back saying, 'Lust doesn't mean attraction to other human beings, it means low desires – of any sort – it's in the general spiritual sense that it's used, not in the common everyday thing.' And – for me – I asked the same question about the anger. I've always felt that it's a release valve – not the best, most positive way, but at least it's *a* way. You know, Karen hates my explosions, because she suffers so much, although they're getting less and less – [*Pete related an instance of how he'd transferred his fury at one situation on to Karen.*]

R: Did she know you'd pushed it over from one thing to the other?

PETE: I suppose she did ... The amazing thing was that it did completely expunge that feeling, letting it out – Although, I feel probably it did damage to my wife's and my relationship, at least I've time to recompense there, as a constant relationship. But without anger sometimes I'd probably get to the point of just literally exploding inwards, which I think would lead to a *massive* giving in. And I suddenly realize that a lot of people haven't the capacity, or – what's the word? The *right* – obvious qualifications to be allowed to explode publicly ... People like you don't explode publicly! Women aren't expected to erupt into massive fits of violence and swearing.

R: I tend to! Not violence – but swearing, anyway –

PETE: Well, you're not expected to! And, say, a young boy from – as you say – a neat family; *his* outbursts – they're not allowed. With kids, sometimes it might even be an argument to occasionally encourage a child to have an outburst, just to get rid of it.

R: I think you *can* be born into the wrong family! What seems normal in some child to other people in a different pattern, is looked on by his own family as abnormal. One point about leaving home is that you go out and choose your friends, and when you're out *there*, with *them*, you've chosen people that you're going to react *with*, but in your family you can be looked on as a monster if you just say something that's not nice!

PETE: If it happens before you've moved away, it can lead to a massive internal collapse. This energy growin' and growin'. And of course a lot of people get into the habit of exploding, and they end up in gaol! If it's left too long undealt with, you collapse inside, and a lot of people give in, completely. I've seen that with a lot of men, particularly in my business, who were insecure, or slightly doubtful – Take, for example, sexual preferences: doubtful about whether they were heterosexual or homosexual – and opt, in the end, for homosexuality in an incredibly defeated state of mind. So then homosexuality becomes labelled as a sickness because people *choose* it, take it on as a sickness. Gives 'em a feeling of actually making a statement – achieving something. And must be very hurtful to the people who're naturally and unashamedly homosexual, you know: being used as this strange sort of test case.

But, as I said before, I don't really understand what leads people to total desperation – [*Pete then described the ups and downs of a great friend, who'd had every form of success, followed by every form of disaster.*] And that's as close as I've come to seeing how somebody can be led, through mistrust, perhaps feeling that you haven't been properly rewarded for your work, to frequent suicide attempts. Very weird to lose a knack, too. With this example, this is something has always bothered me: not to have the feel of the pulse of society; because I don't know what makes me tick, enables me to sit and write a song. Maybe years later I see there was something intuitive – I've got control over the machinery, the structure, but the actual content, you know, what makes it *rich*, I've got no control over at all. It's almost in God's hands, you know. If that goes I've had it.

R: That's the thing about this side of creativity, isn't it?

PETE: I'll be able to do TV commercials! That's it.

R: Like Rossini you might suddenly move over to something different. As he moved over from writing operas to become a chef.

PETE: A chef?! I bet he was a good chef.

R: Don't you think most people live their lives afraid something they're doing will blow up in their faces? Is it important, this, for you?

PETE: I don't brood on it.

R: Were you ever a person who went to books on these occasions? Did you get anything from anywhere but people? Something you read, something you saw maybe; films, on the box –

PETE: I think it's always been me knowin' that music is really the highest possible form of both art and escapism! I'd lived with music since I was a baby. My father was in a successful orchestra called the Squadronnaires. I used to be up in the balcony with Mum, see my Dad down there with his saxophone. Funnily enough, we'd no piano, or anything, so for me it was like – the mouth-organ: used to go and hide with me mouth-organ! I think it was the knowledge that music was – in here – and I could *hear* music; and I could – and do all the time – hear it. It's hearing what is there, you know ... Books: my reading as a child was fairly trivial. There were certain things I read that moved me a lot, and – I always wanted to be a writer! As a kid I wanted to be a journalist –

R: And you've combined both since ... Come out as a second-best side. [*Pete roared.*] I mean, hardly a *second*-best side! More than most people do with one. I'd hate to without music, the final horror would be to be deaf. But there are people who are tone-deaf, or have never had much to do with music, so they haven't got this kind of way into life. Any word you can think of towards people who are desperate, and would be helped by something like that, but just haven't got it?

PETE: For me, I think that the unique thing about Samaritans is the telephone thing – that you can open up to somebody, that initially they don't know who you are. Without getting overly poetic about it, there is a certain similarity within the area of music. You can go and buy a record, listen to a song, it doesn't matter what kind of music you're attracted to, you can hear *in* it the problems, the ups and downs, the ins and outs of the people that wrote it; and to some desperate individuals the sound of just – a listening ear down the other end of the phone, that's a form of music. It's only sound – not contact; it'll never replace a loving embrace, living closely to someone day to day; never replace real children, real relationships – never replace *life* – but it allows the mind to think of something for a second other than itself. And I think this is the time when you're letting your own heart back into your head, as it were. I think people that are really desperate, what they're doing is keeping their heart out of their life, because they're afraid it's going to get hurt – and what they've got to realize is that the heart's completely impregnable. It's the head which is fragile! And if you're completely open and honest – with yourself, most important of all – an' even if you don't understand what's going on, if you just open up at least a part, even to begin with just open up your ears, and see what's there –

R: And with all people, too ... Hazrat Inayat Khan says, somewhere, that everyone gets opportunities every day – but don't even see they're there; having shut their eyes – They want some *big* opportunity, and they want it now. If you just take some step – there's perhaps two opportunities, next time. And that's a sort of – contact.

PETE: I've talked to lots of young kids who've come to see me and say: 'I know I'd be big, if only I got a break.' But I always find myself telling the tale that after sixteen years playing in this Group from pubs right up to stadiums and academy awards, the thing I didn't realize was the key to my life was my own wife and kids, and it took an incredibly hard knock, desperation and loneliness, to realize *that* was under my own nose. Other things had come very easily; *they* weren't the problem. Early on, things I was eager to strive for were simple things which other people had – so I was just as jealous, that they could easily – fall in love, take a job, have a happy family. Maybe it's not so easy, but there are certain simple qualities about so many people that I meet; just the fact, in a sense, that they've already accepted that they might not make it, by saying, 'If I had a break'. There's the 'if'. You see, for me, there was never any 'if'. I was really the most single-minded and conceited person! The whole Group used to think like that!

R: But you worked terrifically hard.

PETE: Hard as we were able to ... But this thing about opportunities: in a sense what comes easily to one person is incredibly difficult to another; and it *has* got to do with being able to see. It's not an art, it's not a trick, to suddenly realize what's the key to your particular life; you can do it, you can see, from the rails that life puts us on. And it's amazing to discover how easy it is to change in a second from being a pessimist about the way things are, to an optimist. And it's acceptance: just accepting the way things are as being not necessarily wonderful, enjoyable things. Not necessarily goin' to make life easier – it might be duff, might be difficult, but who – really – cares? I don't. I accept it the way it is. And *immediately* this process flips everything round – and suddenly *you* are the master. Now and again in my life I've been able to do it, in very difficult situations, and it's just been such a thrill to know that it works – but other times, of course, my moods prevent me from doing it. I say, well, that might work, but I'm not bloody well going to do it, so there.

R: Yes. And it blocks it. That time.

PETE: I suppose an explanation of why that works is because you're accepting your Karmic thing. I'm not really sure the spiritual, or the mystical side, is relevant to something like Samaritans – but I think the great thing about Baba, and even a lot of Sufi teachings, and mystical teachings, and some of the better parts of effective work in Christianity, are that the bits of it that really work, in everyday life, don't necessarily have to have a reason for working – they just simply work.

[*We talked about a girl he knew, who was in a fairly desperate situation, and how a small amount of help given her by a church housing association had made it possible for her to plan a life.*]

PETE: . . . If somebody ever holds out any kind of help, accept it – because in accepting it you're accepting the energy, the love that goes with it, and that's the most precious thing of all.

R: It's a bit of a subtle thing, though – learning how not to swamp once you've accepted ... Some people get to feel very rejected after being helped – they've seen a sort of magic helper who can be drawn on indefinitely, and they don't realize the other person can't involve every bit of their energy in someone else. So much help goes sour when the accepter goes on to say, now – you do this for me, and that, and the other ...

PETE: Well, there was a guy rang me one day who wanted to come and see me, so I met him, and he played me some tapes which I liked; I said that he could go into a studio and record them; and he went – and they were terrible. And he came back in and said, 'The tape's *fantastic*. We've done it, we've done it! We'll go from here, do a solo album; maybe release a single, couple of TVs, then play it by ear. I'll go straight out and get me outfit –' And I sat him down, and explained that what he'd sung to me just on his guitar, on his l'il cassette recorder, was *better*, an' more honest, an' that the whole thing was a waste of time for both of us – And off he went, and we were both back at Square One. It was a sort of futile thing.

I go through this now and again, and it's very sad ... It's also very interesting to look at my mother-in-law after a heavy day on the phone or in the office with a particular person that she's trying to help, come back and be unable to deal at home! Marvellous family, and she's an extremely selfless person. You know, it's an interesting thing to see, as an instance ...

R: ... of not expecting other people to do *all* the dredging up of everything for you?

The tape just then wound to an end. I think we were probably both feeling a little dredged up by that time, anyway. There was nothing really that I could add to the interview, except to thank Pete warmly for his help – and perhaps to end the article with a few more words from Thoreau, possibly worth remembering in a difficult job or family situation: 'What old people say you cannot do, you try and find that you can.'

The Soldier

ROALD DAHL

So much damage has been done to this man by the war that he is losing control of his body as well as his mind. He cannot feel hot or cold, hard or soft. The door knob changes sides. Someone who is not there follows him when he walks the dog at night. The sound of a plane paralyses him, waiting for the bomb's whistle-shriek.

This is a story of fear and pain. We share the wife's fear and the man's pain, each of them alone with the other, each alone with themselves. A horror story told with pity.

MONICA DICKENS

＊

It was one of those nights that made him feel he knew what it was like to be a blind man: not the shadow of an image for his eyes to discern, not even the forms of the trees visible against the sky.

Out of the darkness he became aware of small rustling noises in the hedge, the breathing of a horse some distance away in the field, the soft thud of a hoof as it moved its foot; and once he heard the rush of a bird flying past him low overhead.

'Jock,' he said, speaking loud. 'We'll go home now.' And he turned and began to walk back up the slope of the lane, the dog pulling ahead, showing the way in the dark.

It must be nearly midnight, he thought. That meant that soon it would be tomorrow. Tomorrow was worse than today. Tomorrow was the worst of all because it was going to become today – and today was now.

Today had not been very nice, especially that business with the splinter.

Stop it, he told himself. There isn't any sense thinking about it. It doesn't do anyone any good thinking about things like that. Think about something else for a change. You can kick out a dangerous thought, you know, if you put another in its place. Go right back as far as you can go. Let's have some memories of sweet days. The seaside holidays in the summer, wet sand and red buckets and shrimping nets and the slippery seaweedy rocks and the small clear pools and sea anemones and snails and mussels and sometimes one grey translucent shrimp hovering deep down in the beautiful green water.

But how *could* that splinter have got into the sole of his foot without him feeling it?

It is not important. Do you remember hunting for cowries along the margin of the tide, each one so fine and perfect it became a precious jewel to be held in the hand all the way home; and the little orange-coloured scallops, the pearly oyster shells, the tiny bits of emerald glass, a live hermit crab, a cockle, the spine of a skate, and once, but never to be forgotten, the dry seawashed jawbone of a human being with teeth in it, white and wonderful among the shells and pebbles. Oh Mummy, look what I've found! Look, Mummy, look!

But to go back to the splinter. She had really been rather unpleasant about that.

'What do you mean, you didn't notice?' she had asked, scornful.

'I just didn't notice, that's all.'

'I suppose you're going to tell me if I stick a pin into your foot you won't feel it?'

'I didn't say that.'

And then she had jabbed him suddenly in the ankle with the pin she had been using to take out the splinter, and he hadn't been watching so he didn't know about it till she had cried out in a kind of horror. And when he had looked down, the pin was sticking into the flesh all by itself behind the ankle-bone, almost half of it buried.

'Take it out,' he had said. 'You can poison someone like that.'

'You mean you can't *feel* it?'

'Take it out, will you?'

'You mean it doesn't hurt?'

'The pain is terrible. Take it out.'

'What's the *matter* with you?'

'I said the pain is terrible. Didn't you hear me?'

Why did they *do* things like that to him?

When I was down beside the sea, a wooden spade they gave to me, to dig the sandy shore. My holes were empty as a cup, and every time the sea came up, till it could come no more.

A year ago the doctor had said, 'Shut your eyes. Now tell me whether I'm pushing this toe up or down.'

'Up,' he had said.

'And now?'

'Down. No, up. I think it's up.'

It was peculiar that a neuro-surgeon should want to play with his toes.

'Did I get them all right, doctor?'

'You did very well.'

But that was a year ago. He had felt pretty good a year ago. The sort of things that happened now never used to happen then. Take, for example, just one item – the bathroom tap.

Why was the hot tap in the bathroom on a different side this morning? That was a new one.

It is not of the least importance, you understand, but it would be interesting to know why.

Do you think she could have changed it over, taken a spanner and a pipe-wrench and sneaked in during the night and changed it over?

Do you? Well – if you really want to know – yes. The way she's been acting lately, she'd be quite capable of doing that.

A strange and difficult woman, that's what she was. Mind you, she used not to be, but there's no doubt at all that right now she was as strange and difficult as they come. Especially at night.

Yes, at night. That was the worst time of all – the night.

Why, when he put out his right hand in bed at night, could his fingers not feel what they were touching? He had knocked over the lamp and she had woken up and then sat up suddenly while he was feeling for it on the floor in the dark.

'What are you doing now?'

'I knocked over the lamp. I'm sorry.'

'Oh Christ,' she had said. 'Yesterday it was the glass of water. What's the *matter* with you?'

Once, the doctor had stroked the back of his hand with a feather, and he hadn't been able to feel that either. But he had felt it when the man scratched him with a pin.

'Shut your eyes. No – you mustn't look. Shut them tight. Now tell me if this is hot or cold.'

'Hot.'

'And this?'

'Cold.'

'And this?'

'Cold. I mean hot. Yes, it's hot, isn't it?'

'That's right,' the doctor had said. 'You did very well.'

But that was a year ago.

Why were the switches on the walls, just lately, always a few inches away from the well-remembered places when he felt for them in the dark?

Don't think about it, he told himself. The only thing is not to think about it.

And while we're on the subject, why did the walls of the living-room take on a slightly different shade of colour each day?

Green and blue-green and blue; and sometimes – sometimes slowly swimming like colours seen through the heat-haze of a brazier.

One by one, neatly, like index cards out of a machine, the little questions dropped.

Whose face appeared for one second at the window during dinner? Whose eyes?

'What are you staring at?'

'Nothing,' he had answered. 'But it would be nice if we could draw the curtains, don't you think?'

'Robert, what were you staring at?'

'Nothing.'

'Why were you staring at the window like that?'

'It would be nice if we could draw the curtains, don't you think?' he had answered.

He was going past the place where he had heard the horse in the field and now he could hear it again: the breathing, the soft hoof thuds, and the crunch of grass-cropping that was like the noise of a man munching celery.

'Hello old horse,' he said, calling loud into the darkness. 'Hello old horse over there.'

Suddenly he heard the footsteps behind him, slow, long striding footsteps close behind, and he stopped. The footsteps stopped. He turned around, searching the darkness.

'Good evening,' he said. 'You here again?'

In the quiet that followed he could hear the wind moving the leaves in the hedge.

'Are you going my way?' he said.

Then he turned and walked on, the dog still pulling ahead, and the footsteps started after him again, but more softly now, as though the person were walking on toes.

He stopped and turned again.

'I can't see you,' he said, 'because it's so dark. Are you someone I know?'

Again the silence, and the cool summer wind on his

cheeks, and the dog tugging on the leash to get home.

'All right,' he called. 'You don't have to answer if you don't want to. But remember I know you're there.'

Someone trying to be clever.

Far away in the night, over to the west and very high, he heard the faint hum of an aeroplane. He stopped again, head up, listening.

'Miles away,' he said. 'Won't come near here.'

But why, when one of them flew over the house, did everything inside him come to a stop, and his talking and what he was doing, while he sat or stood in a sort of paralysis waiting for the whistle-shriek of the bomb. That one after dinner this evening.

'Why did you duck like that?' she had asked.

'Duck?'

'Why did you duck? What are you ducking for?'

'Duck?' he had said again. 'I don't know what you mean.'

'I'll say you don't,' she had answered, staring at him hard with those hard, blue-white eyes, the lids dropping slightly, as always when there was contempt. The drop of her eyelids was something beautiful to him, the half-closed eyes and the way the lids dropped and the eyes became hooded when her contempt was extreme.

Yesterday, lying in bed in the early morning, when the noise of gunfire was just beginning far away down the valley, he had reached out with his left hand and touched her body for a little comfort.

'What on earth are you doing?'

'Nothing, dear.'

'You woke me up.'

'I'm sorry.'

It would be a help if she would only let him lie closer to her in the early mornings when he began to hear the noise of gun-fire.

He would soon be home now. Around the last bend of the

lane he could see a light glowing pink through the curtain of the living-room window, and he hurried forward to the gate and through it and up the path to the front door, the dog still pulling ahead.

It was on the right when he went out. He distinctly remembered it being on the right-hand side when he shut the door half an hour ago and went out.

It couldn't be that she had changed *that* over too? Just to fox him? Taken a bag of tools and quickly changed it over to the other side while he was out walking the dog?

He moved his hand over to the left – and the moment the fingers touched the knob, something small but violent exploded inside his head and with it a surge of fury and outrage and fear. He opened the door, shut it quickly behind him and shouted 'Edna, are you there?'

There was no answer so he shouted again, and this time she heard him.

'What do you want now? You woke me up.'

'Come down here a moment, will you. I want to talk to you.'

'Oh for heaven's sake,' she answered. 'Be quiet and come on up.'

'Come here!' he shouted. 'Come here at once!'

'I'll be damned if I will. You come here.'

The man paused, head back, looking up the stairs into the dark of the second floor. He could see where the stair-rail curved to the left and went on up out of sight in the black towards the landing and if you went straight on across the landing you came to the bedroom, and it would be black in there too.

'Edna!' he shouted. 'Edna!'

'Oh go to hell.'

He began to move slowly up the stairs, treading quietly, touching the stair-rail for guidance, up and around the left-hand curve into the dark above. At the top he took an extra

step that wasn't there; but he was ready for it and there was
no noise. He paused awhile then, listening, and he wasn't
sure, but he thought he could hear the guns starting up again
far away down the valley, heavy stuff mostly, seventy-fives and
maybe a couple of mortars somewhere in the background.

Across the landing now and through the open doorway –
which was easy in the dark because he knew it so well –
through on to the bedroom carpet that was thick and soft and
pale grey although he could not feel or see it.

In the centre of the room he waited, listening for sounds.
She had gone back to sleep and was breathing rather loud,
making the slightest little whistle with the air between her
teeth each time she exhaled. The curtain flapped gently
against the open window, the alarm-clock tick-tick-ticked
beside the bed.

Now that his eyes were becoming accustomed to the dark
he could just make out the end of the bed, the white blanket
tucked in under the mattress, the bulge of her feet under the
bedclothes; and then, as though aware of the presence of the
man in the room, the woman stirred. He heard her turn, and
turn again. The sound of her breathing stopped. There was a
succession of little movement-noises and once the bedsprings
creaked, loud as a shout in the dark.

'Is that you Robert?'

He made no move, no sound.

'Robert, are you there?'

The voice was strange and rather unpleasant to him.

'Robert!' She was wide awake now. 'Where are you?'

Where had he heard that voice before? It had a quality of
stridence, dissonance, like two single high notes struck
together hard in discord. Also there was an inability to pro-
nounce the R of Robert. Who was it that used to say Wobert
to him?

'Wobert,' she said again. 'What are you doing?'

Was it that nurse in the hospital, the tall one with fair

hair? No, it was further back. Such an awful voice as that he ought to remember. Give him a little time and he would get the name.

At that moment he heard the snap of the switch of the bedside lamp and in the flood of light he saw the woman half-sitting up in bed, dressed in some sort of a pink nightdress. There was a surprised, wide-eyed expression on her face. Her cheeks and chin were oily with cold cream.

'You better put that thing down,' she was saying, 'before you cut yourself.'

'Where's Edna?' He was staring at her hard.

The woman, half-sitting up in bed, watched him carefully. He was standing at the foot of the bed, a huge, broad man, standing motionless, erect, with heels together, almost at attention, dressed in his dark-brown, woolly, heavy suit.

'Go on,' she ordered. 'Put it down.'

'Where's Edna?'

'What's the matter with you, Wobert?'

'There's nothing the matter with me. I'm just asking you where's my wife?'

The woman was easing herself up gradually into an erect sitting position and sliding her legs towards the edge of the bed. 'Well,' she said at length, the voice changing, the hard blue-white eyes secret and cunning, 'if you really want to know, Edna's gone. She left just now while you were out.'

'Where did she go?'

'She didn't say.'

'And who are you?'

'I'm just a friend of hers.'

'You don't have to shout at me,' he said. 'What's all the excitement?'

'I simply want you to know I'm not Edna.'

The man considered this a moment, then he said, 'How did you know my name?'

'Edna told me.'

Again he paused, studying her closely, still slightly puzzled, but much calmer now, his eyes calm, perhaps even a little amused the way they looked at her.

'I think I prefer Edna.'

In the silence that followed they neither of them moved. The woman was very tense, sitting up straight with her arms tense on either side of her and slightly bent at the elbows, the hands pressing palms downward on the mattress.

'I love Edna, you know. Did she ever tell you I love her?'

The woman didn't answer.

'I think she's a bitch. But it's a funny thing I love her just the same.'

The woman was not looking at the man's face; she was watching his right hand.

'Awful cruel little bitch, Edna.'

And a long silence now, the man standing erect, motionless, the woman sitting motionless in the bed, and it was so quiet suddenly that through the open window they could hear the water in the millstream going over the dam far down the valley on the next farm.

Then the man again, speaking calmly, slowly, quite impersonally:

'As a matter of fact, I don't think she even likes me any more.'

The woman shifted closer to the edge of the bed. 'Put that knife down,' she said, 'before you cut yourself.'

'Don't shout, please. Can't you talk nicely?' Now, suddenly, the man leaned forward, staring intently into the woman's face, and he raised his eyebrows. 'That's strange,' he said. 'That's very strange.'

He took a step forward, his knees touching the bed.

'You look a bit like Edna yourself.'

'Edna's gone out. I told you that.'

He continued to stare at her and the woman kept quite still, the palms of her hands pressing deep into the mattress.

'Well,' he said. 'I wonder.'

'I told you Edna's gone out. I'm a friend of hers. My name is Mary.'

'My wife,' the man said, 'has a funny little brown mole just behind her left ear. You don't have that, do you?'

'I certainly don't.'

'Turn your head and let me look.'

'I told you I didn't have it.'

'Just the same, I'd like to make sure.'

The man came slowly around the end of the bed. 'Stay where you are,' he said. 'Please don't move.' And he came towards her slowly, watching her all the time, a little smile touching the corners of his mouth.

The woman waited until he was within reach, and then, with a quick right hand, so quick he never even saw it coming, she smacked him hard across the front of the face. And when he sat down on the bed and began to cry, she took the knife from his hand and went swiftly out of the room, down the stairs to the hall, where the telephone was.

Poems

BRIAN PATTEN

The world is full of lonely people, longing for companionship, dying, sometimes literally, for someone to talk to. Beyond the uncertain awkward things like 'dating bars' and 'singles clubs' and 'computer pairing', no one has figured out a way to bring together the lonely ones who need each other. 'Making a Call' (page 9) suggests one way, wistfully, hopefully . . .

In 'If You Had to Hazard . . .' the poet reminds us that people make their own lives, 'invent their own ugliness'. He speaks to the frail egos who 'lie in ambush for themselves' to prevent themselves from allowing themselves to like themselves, and to be free and have fun.

He speaks to the suicidal. Chosen self-condemnation is closely linked to chosen self-destruction.

MONICA DICKENS

*

'IF YOU HAD TO HAZARD A GUESS, WHO WOULD YOU SAY YOUR POETRY IS FOR?'

For people who have nowhere to go in the afternoons,
    for people who the evening banishes to small rooms,
for good people, people huge as the world.
    For people who give themselves away forgetting
what it is they are giving,
    and who are never reminded.
For people who cannot help being kind
    to the hand bunched in pain against them.
For inarticulate people,

  people who invent their own ugliness,
who invent pain, terrified of blankness;
  and for people who stand forever at the same junctions
waiting for the chances that have passed.
  And for people who lie in ambush for themselves,
  who invent toughness as a kind of disguise,
who, lost in their narrow and self-defeating worlds,
carry remorse inside them like a plague;
and for the self-seeking self lost among them
  I hazard a poem.

SOMEWHERE BETWEEN HEAVEN AND WOOLWORTH'S

A Song

She keeps kingfishers in their cages
And goldfish in their bowls,
She is lovely and is afraid
Of such things as growing cold.

She's had enough men to please her
Though they were more cruel than kind
And their love an act in isolation,
A form of pantomime.

She says she has forgotten
The feelings that she shared
At various all-night parties
Among the couples on the stairs,

For among the songs and dancing
She was once open wide,
A girl dressed in denim
With boys dressed in lies.

She's eating roses on toast with tulip butter,
Praying for her mirror to stay young;
On its no longer gilted surface
This message she has scrawled:

'O somewhere between Heaven and Woolworth's
I live I love I scold,
I keep kingfishers in their cages
And goldfish in their bowls.'

IN NUMEROUS CITY GARDENS

... And in numerous city gardens
Long legged girls left alone, bow low among the trees,
Heavy with morning sickness
They wish to be eaten by the sun
And to disappear;
And their hair blown blond or black or brown,
Falls across their faces like waterfalls,
And the gardeners know them, those girls
Who break down by the summer houses into tears,
Who left empty now
Wish the boys who have left them to come near.

Lethargically and without much effort
They count on their fingers
The days that are fading,
Lost in their own isolation
They see in each face a continent of sadness
As the secretaries, potent in the sunlight,
And their men, drift past them.
And like children lost in fading grottoes
They see behind transparent cities

Sad empty visions
And detach themselves from living for a while.

*

And now that your heart is able to share in their isolation
What can you possibly see
But an army of days moving towards their end
And those things decay
You thought could not have decayed?
So come close now, and sighing, join in the parade;
Our lives must move gently on the world,
And huddled together for comfort and for ease
Let us note in separate ways
How we are lost in our isolation
And count on our fingers
The passing of days.

I Am Lonely
JOAN AIKEN

To be deluded does not mean to be illogical. The thinking of the man in this story is at the same time deranged and rational. His unreal belief about himself is explained and justified. Things other people say and do seem to illustrate and confirm what only he knows.

Only to him. This disturbing tale shows how when the mind slides over the edge of what we call sanity, the victim still has a grasp on reality — but it's a different reality from everyone else's.

MONICA DICKENS

*

I was in the hotel lounge with a book to prevent people speaking to me, for when they speak to me, unless I am very much on my guard, it hurts me. It makes it, you see, like the time before Ailsa went away. Of course Ailsa did more than speak, far more, but she did speak to me with her tongue and her larynx ... And so I avoid being spoken to as much as I can. I like to be just myself, in myself, like a nut inside its hard shell, and that is lonely but I prefer it, because I don't like to be reminded of the time before Ailsa went away. Some people think that we shall see each other again, and some don't, and that makes it all the more terrifying, because I don't know which to believe. So when I can I concentrate on just being a nut inside its hard shell, and the best place for that is in the hotel lounge with a book.

At first I was not reading it. I leaned back in my chair looking at it, but all the time I was acutely aware of the people around me. There was George. He was sitting very upright and slim and composed, smoking, and looking straight ahead of him through his thick white eyelashes. Two girls were playing double patience on the sofa, and the whole evening they kept up a running mutter. 'No, Jenny, you should have put the ten on the jack, then you could have moved over the queen.' 'Wait, you've forgotten that seven.' One of them was plump, with an amiable silly face, and whenever she made a mistake she said 'Oh I am so sorry,' and giggled, while the other one sighed with impatience.

Directly behind me someone was reading the paper, and every now and then he read out a scrap from it. A man in another armchair was writing letters, thoughtfully adding a phrase from time to time and then leaning back, looking at the ceiling and thinking. He had brown eyes and they would suddenly harden as he remembered something. His cigarette lay in the ashtray beside him, and it was nothing but a long cylinder of ash. A nervous woman was blinking and knitting. There were other people all round me. One of them had a bad cough.

I didn't need to look at them to know they were there, because the life from them ran out and battered against my shell like little scratching hands, and I felt like laughing because I was so much aware in the middle of them, and yet I was almost invisible.

Then all of a sudden I began to remember that I was myself and I felt a terrible wave of despair coming up towards me. I waited for it. One can't run away from that, because it is everywhere, like poisoned air. The music from the wireless changed and I recognized it. It was the second movement of Beethoven's First Symphony, and it is a fugue. The last time I had heard it was long ago in the summer. I had been out with Ailsa. We had been for a picnic, and we walked back along the road talking, and as we came near the end of the walk we went more and more slowly because it was such a beautiful evening and we wanted it not to end. I can't remember what we talked about. One hardly ever can, that is the curious thing. Although the only important moments of my life are the ones I spent talking to Ailsa, I can only think of about four or five of the things she said, and those are not the vital ones. Ridiculous remarks, some of them are, when we were too happy to be serious. I can remember – but I am not keeping to the point, and I must do that, to explain how all this happened. I listened to the second movement of Beethoven's First Symphony and I remembered our picnic. Very clearly. I could even smell the grass of the field where we lay, which was so dry that it was very nearly hay, and I could remember the way the long grasses arched across the sky when we lay on our backs and looked up, and the mallow and willowherb and bedstraw along the banks of the road, and how the wild roses in the hedge were dusty and tangled with strands of hay. And how the larks sang and the smell of a July evening.

I sat and remembered all this. No, I did more than remember it, I lived it again with every bone in my body. I put my face down on the arm of the chair and trembled because I was so happy. I was overflowing with gratitude; I almost said *thank you*, in case there was anyone who was responsible. I had not then realized the truth. I wanted to laugh. I felt confident. I knew that I was safe. And all the time I was remembering Ailsa, and it was as if she were in the room with me.

I lifted my head from my arm and stared straight ahead of me. I wanted to attract the attention of the man with the sad brown eyes who was writing a letter but he had rested his forehead on his hands and was looking at the floor. He never looked up. All at once I stopped wanting to laugh. I felt very cold and strange as if I were a statue on top of a pedestal. I looked at him leaning his forehead on his hand and then I looked round the room at all the people, sitting or standing in groups. The room was very full. I no longer felt happy. I wondered – if I will myself, can I feel that happiness again?

Perhaps I will. But I refused to let myself try and I was pleased with myself for refusing. That sort of thing is cowardly. I kept my head up and looked in front of me and presently I began to notice the people in the room again.

All this time, you understand, they had been there, playing patience and talking and writing letters and knitting and smoking. But I had forgotten them. Now they all crowded back one by one, on to the path of my mind, like beads on to a string.

'Do you tell a lot of lies?' one girl asked another. 'Oh, a lot,' she answered. 'How many in a week?' 'Oh, I don't know. I wouldn't like to guess.' Someone stretched and went out. Two men were talking. 'Of course if you like that sort of thing,' one them said, and the other one answered, 'But you see one has to make allowances. Personally I think it is just a lot of –' They laughed and looked supercilious.

The room was so full that it was like a clock ticking. There was a hum of life going on all the time, not a hum of talk but a mechanical vibration as all these personalities met and passed each other by. They were all cogs and the room was part of some vast organism.

The man with the brown eyes folded up his letter and put it into an envelope which he addressed. And then, suddenly, as he was rising to his feet, pushing himself slowly out of his chair, the realization struck me.

I expect you will think I was foolish not to have known it before. But it does take some getting used to. I expect I was too much engrossed in Ailsa to notice it. And before Ailsa? Before Ailsa was like before being drunk: the state of being drunk seems to progress backwards in time until one's birth.

At any rate, as I sat there among these human cogs I knew in a flash that I was god. At first I did not understand all that it meant. And then slowly I saw that if I was god I could do anything.

I tried at first tentatively. I made the woman who was

knitting drop her wool. Then I made her pull out a knitting needle. Then I tried someone else. I made George get up and put his cigarette case on the mantelpiece. I began to be fascinated. Moving them about was like playing chess, only a thousand times more interesting and complicated. I had to be alert all the time, to manipulate all the brains at once.

I know. You are going to ask a question. You are going to say, But how did it all get done before? Well, I am not going to answer that now. It was asking questions that began the disaster. But I haven't got there yet.

I sat in the lounge and I felt very calm and very happy. Not happy in the same way as before; that sort of happiness doesn't come often and it doesn't stay long. But all the same, there was something of that happiness in me: it was like all the hot liquid fires that run about in the centre of the world compressed into one cool shining diamond.

I sat very upright and attended to the business of moving those people about, and making them stay alive. Because of course if I had let go of them they would have collapsed like so many heaps of empty clothes. It was a terrifying thought, that, in a way: I was responsible for so much, and there was no one to help me. But as well as being terrifying it was exhilarating. I stood up and strolled over to the window and looked at the people in the street, to see what they were doing. I know, you are going to ask another question, but I shan't answer it. Why should I give away my professional secrets.

I stood and looked out. It was raining. The pavements shone. Across the street there was a small boy walking along very carefully on the slippery pavement, and in his arms he was holding a kitten. It was very draggled and seemed to be frightened: it clung to him with all its claws. I watched him as he went slowly by, and then I used my power to make him slip and fall down.

The kitten sprang out of his grasp in alarm, and skittered

away to the corner. He picked himself up, and he was rather muddy and had a cut knee. I saw him rub away tears from his eyes with his muddy knuckle before he started away round the corner in pursuit of the kitten.

And then I felt sorry for him. That movement of his, which was so resigned and determined as he rubbed his eyes and set off to look for the kitten, hurt me terribly. And I thought, What does this mean? I am god. I can't be hurt by anything. But the thought of the little boy who had fallen down and lost his kitten kept on nagging at me, because I had done it and I was sorry I had done it. And it didn't seem to me that god could be sorry for something he had done.

Thinking about that worried me because I couldn't solve it. So I turned away from the window and went back to my armchair to watch the people in the room. They were all listening intently to the nine o'clock news. I saw from their faces that it was bad and I thought, I'll do something about that soon, when I have plenty of time. I tied a knot in my handkerchief to remind myself. The brown-eyed man was standing by the door with his letters, listening to the end of the bulletin; then he went out. I followed him. I was tired of all those people in the room. I didn't care very much if they all fell down like empty sacks after I had gone out. They probably did; after all, if you stop to think, what else could they do? Naturally when I go back into the room they all come to life again. It is like looking at yourself in a mirror. Whenever you look at your eyes they are staring straight at you.

In the hall I met a man whom I used to know a long time ago. I never liked him. He wrote – hard, varnished stuff; he was very successful.

He came up to me now and said hullo. I was polite to him, and that was strange because if I had liked I could have blasted him where he stood. But I asked him how he was. He told me that he was fine. He had been appointed to the editorship of some paper and he was proud of that. I could have laughed at him with his silly little piece of vanity.

Then he said, 'What about you? Are you still writing?'

'No,' I said, 'I've given that up.' I didn't tell him that I was god.

'That's good,' he said. 'You'd never have made a success of it.' He smiled at me in a superior way, but I had nothing to say, I was so angry and so hurt that I just drew in my breath and stared at him. I could have made him fall dead at my feet. But I did not. Because I was god and I was far above him.

The next thing that I remember is walking down the steps into the street. I was tired, terribly tired, and I wanted to go to sleep. I thought that perhaps I could go into the park and sit on a chair and go to sleep. But suddenly a terrible thought struck me. I expect you will have thought of it, but I hadn't. Of course, god never sleeps. For if he slept, what would happen to the solar system, and the growing plants, and the trees, and the tides, and the traffic? The whole universe would collapse. The very thought made me shiver, but I was horribly worried, for I was so sleepy, and I did not know how I could manage to stay awake for the rest of my life: god's life. Eternity.

I turned back. The streets seemed changed, different, and I couldn't think of anywhere to go but the hotel. So I went back there.

It was emptying when I climbed the steps again. People went away in little groups, hurrying to their appointments. There were only two people in the lounge, a man and a woman, and they were very intent on each other, talking with brilliant eyes. They were arguing.

The woman suddenly jumped up and said, 'Come outside and I'll show you. It's wonderful,' and when she stood up she had a kind of wiry thinness like a cat's, that reminded me of Ailsa. Ailsa was like a cat in some ways. Not one of those fat, pampered cats, but a sleek, healthy cat, which walks very lithely. You can almost feel the muscles under its smooth fur. The man and woman went out together and all of a sudden I realized that I was alone. The room was empty and I stood in the middle of it and thought of Ailsa. She wasn't there. She was nowhere there.

Then I began again wondering which were right, those who said we should never meet again or the others? Ailsa, you see, was run over and killed a week ago. And then I suddenly remembered that I was god, and that this day would go on for eternity. There is no afterwards unless this is afterwards.

I sat down to think it all out.

Being god, I don't notice time as ordinary people do, or space. I am not certain, for instance, when I came here. This room, I must say, seems more suitable for god. It is very light, quite frighteningly light. As a matter of fact I prefer its being light; I find it easier to stay awake. The walls are white, absolutely white, except for a spider in one corner. Sometimes I make him run up and down his web. I am not interested in the world just now. By and by I shall have another look at it – not now. I am sick of it all, of the responsibility. If only I dared go to sleep that would be perfect. Then I should be happy again, as god ought to be – or at least I should forget that I am unhappy.

I am unhappy because if I am god I ought to be able to find Ailsa. But I don't know where to look for her. And I am so very lonely.

Teenage Depression
MARGARET FORSTER

This young girl is suffering from depression, that terrible heavy, hopeless state that can hit any of us at any age, but seems most threatening at the opposite ends of life, youth and old age.

It can come for no apparent reason, like a black cloud descending. It slows down life. It makes everything pointless. It smothers confidence and joy in being. Its two worst effects are that it isolates the sufferer from other people, and it seems as if it will go on for ever.

This is particularly affecting because the girl is the writer herself, and she is telling very honestly, and with an uncanny memory for exact details, what it was actually like. The misery hit her when she was fifteen, and lasted for two years. She pulled herself out of it by sheer willpower.

Many people can't. But more and more is now known about depression as an illness with physical causes, and there are specific drugs which almost always help. And anyone who feels like the girl in this story can call the Samaritans to discuss how to surmount it. Depression does not need to be for ever.

MONICA DICKENS

*

When I was fifteen years old I used to go to bed at half past six even on a brilliantly sunny summer's evening. I would solemnly undress, get into bed, put my arms behind my head and stare at the hideous flowered wallpaper. I hated that room – it symbolized all that was wrong with my life. Instead of the gay little bed-sittingroom I fancied where there would be bunks and shelves for books and cushions scattered around in bright primary colours and white walls and a thick rug for me to curl up on and a pine desk with hundreds of drawers – instead, there was a large double bed which I had to share with my younger sister, an enormous wardrobe, an elderly dressing table and a chest for putting blankets in. These incredibly ugly post-war bits of utility furniture fought for space in the narrow path round the bed and they were simply beyond disguise. The room was always freezing cold but there was no heating of any kind. It was the dreariest room in the world but I retreated voluntarily to it as early as I could.

Below, I could hear the familiar sounds of normal family life. The radio was on, my mother and sister moved around chatting, my father was outside in his garden digging and in the side alley my brother struggled to clean and mend his bicycle. They had all long ago given up asking me if I was ill. Ostentatiously I would gather up my things the minute tea was over and say 'Well, I'm off.' They raised eyebrows to each other but no longer tried to persuade me to stay. Only my father's anger remained a constant factor and he would have stopped me if my mother had allowed him to, but she would not. 'Oh, let her go,' she would say sorrowfully 'if it makes her happy.' But it didn't. Hour after hour I would stare straight in front of me, watching the shadows lengthen as the light faded, and I would think give me three good reasons why I should stay alive. Sometimes I would cry, without wiping the tears away, and often I would talk to myself. 'Come on, clever clogs,' I would say, 'just three good reasons.'

What I remember most vividly about that awful period is that I could never think of even one reason that was convincing. Obsessed with needing reasons, I used to shout in the middle of arguments at other times 'Why – just tell me why – why was I ever born?' My poor sweet mother would either look bewildered or else lower her head and mumble, 'Because I wanted you.' 'What? What?' I would yell back, pausing for hyena-like laughter, 'What do you mean, you wanted me?

Why did you want me? What was the point? Go on – What was the point?' She never replied. She was gentle where I was violent, and peace-loving where I was belligerent. She just sighed and looked sad and made me scream all over again, 'What was the point of having me? Why was I ever born?'

The need for some clearly defined purpose in my life drove me crazy. I couldn't accept that I, together with millions of others, was just the product of sex. It had, in my opinion, to be more deliberate than that. Surely I couldn't have been created just to wither away my existence like everyone I saw around me? The dullness of their lives shocked me and depressed me more than anything. Look at my mother – up at six-thirty, light the boiler, black the grate, make breakfast, wash the clothes, shop, cook dinner, wash the dishes, iron, mend and put her curlers in at eleven o'clock at night. Great. Treats consisted of Holy Communion on Sunday. Life was one long grind and there was no sense in it. Even for those women better off than my mother it was simply a case of going nowhere only going in greater comfort and style. Everywhere I looked there seemed to be the same boring pattern – women everywhere breeding and slaving for husbands and children and for what?

Bit by bit, I had convinced myself I was trapped. I too would end up on the same conveyor belt. Nothing glorious and wonderful would ever happen to me – that glittering world I saw outside would pass me by. What threatened to panic me was the almost daily proof of my ordinariness. How could I get out? How could I become part of that other world I read about in books and saw at the pictures? There seemed to me no comparison between what I wanted and what I had. An image returned again and again to torment me – an image of me looking down on myself on the bed, then zooming away and looking at the house, the street, the town, the country, the world – all the time tiny me, a mere speck now, receding until only I knew I was there at all. I only had to blink and I lost sight of myself, and a kind of terror overtook me at my own insignificance.

I never talked about my fears, but then talk of that description never happened in our house. Often, I was asked what on earth was the matter with me but nobody seemed even remotely interested in finding out. Even if they had, there was the impossibility of putting into words my muddled thoughts. So I remained just an extremely moody teenager to my family. I got up, went to school, came home, went to bed, slept and got up again to another day in which nothing ever happened. It could only get worse as far as I could see. The greyness grew worse, the sense of futility overwhelmed me and a physical exhaustion set in that almost convinced my mother I had leukemia. Why not end it all now, I found myself thinking, why not cut out all this waiting for death – which was all life was after all. Once done, I would know nothing about it. Oblivion, that was all, no more worrying no more trying to work things out, just nothing.

I never went so far as to try to commit suicide but I thought about it a lot. The trouble was that although I approved of the idea in theory, I was afraid of pain. If I had had access to sleeping pills or tranquillizers, I have a feeling I might just at one point have made some kind of dramatic gesture, but, since I did not, slashed wrists terrified me. Besides, it would be dreadful for the person who found me and I could not see any way round that. The thought of one of my family finding me in a pool of blood was horrifying, though I was in love with what would happen next – there I would lie in a coffin surrounded by flowers and they would all wring their hands and wonder why this young and tender girl had taken her own life. My note would hardly enlighten them since I intended to be cryptic if not downright obscure in my best pompous style. And really, they would all secretly admire me because I would have done what they all wanted to do and didn't dare.

I think, looking back, that my worst misfortune was to conceal the extent of my unhappiness. I don't think I appeared unhappy so much as difficult. I glared, I sulked, I stormed, I raged, I argued – but I didn't look or sound sad in any recognizable way. I seemed, I suspect, extremely confident and arrogant and contemptuous and no one suspected that what I wanted most of all was reassurance. If I had been gentle and wistful and shy and all those more attractive qualities perhaps someone would have had the sense to put their arms round me and enlighten me. They could have told me what I needed to know – that my mother's life, for example, just looked like drudgery but wasn't to her. I was on the outside looking into a way of life I didn't understand. That daily routine I so despised was a source of happiness to my mother but I couldn't recognize the rhythms – I couldn't appreciate that events so mundane were what she wanted. There wasn't any need to pity her, nor to fear becoming like her.

Nor were matters helped by my obstinate refusal to have anything to do with the rest of the human race. I was lonely, but would never have admitted it – indeed, I made a feature of it. Proudly, I chose to be alone when company was available and said that I liked it and encouraged everyone to think that I was the cat who walked by herself. To a certain extent it was true – I did like being on my own – but though it may seem a contradiction, I was at the same time lonely. Stuck in my introspective groove, I successfully shut out any chance of that state of affairs altering. I scorned all invitations. My view of life was so cynical (and yet at the same time so romantic) that I saw through all social occasions for the puny things they were. I wanted only the best and wasn't prepared to give second rate a chance from which something better might come. Other girls in my class might go to parties but I would not – the parties I craved were colourful, exotic gatherings not squalid thrashes in someone's overcrowded drab sitting room. Other girls went out with boys – but not I, for I wanted handsome, tanned, sophisticated escorts not pimply faced callow youths. And so, because of my scorn, friends became afraid to ask me to anything. I would only sneer. I would only ask what was the point. My sourness would only turn any event into a disaster. Gradually, I forced upon myself a position I did not want to be in and I became one of those strange people, not quite like anyone else, that everyone was afraid of. My attitude said leave me alone and the more I was left alone the easier it became to pretend that was what I wanted.

It would be nice to say that I was rescued from this predicament by some single event, or by some wise person, but it wasn't like that. Getting out of my slough of despond was very gradual and inevitably humiliating. It became, in the end, absolutely unbearable to be surrounded at school by scores of girls all of whom seemed to be having endless fun. Life, so far as I could see, was one long round of pleasure, from which I had excluded myself. I saw that unless I was prepared to swallow my cutting words and subject myself to experiences I had pushed aside I was never going to make any progress. 'Oh all right then,' I said ungraciously one day, 'I'll come to your stupid party, but don't expect me to stay long – I'll come to your silly Youth Club but I'll probably walk straight out – I'll go on that outing but don't expect me to enjoy it.' And I didn't. The party, the club, the outing, they were all as inadequate as I had imagined. But they were better than staring at wallpaper and afterwards it was entertaining to be able to criticize. Finally, I had something to do, something to rush off to, some possibility however remote of something happening, and that, more than anything, helped conquer suicidal depression.

It must be very rare indeed that anyone is lifted out of a depression by the action of someone else, particularly if that depression is not based on something concrete. I had nothing, after all, to be depressed about in theory – good home, good health, nothing nasty happening in the woodshed. The only thing that would get me out of my misery was a change in my attitude. It seems to be that I learned the hard way that you have to take the crumbs when what you want is the cake – or something like that. You have to go forth and expose your own naked need when what you want to do is curl up and die. You have to stop thinking nothing nice will ever happen and give it a chance to happen.

Around the age of seventeen I came out of that long, long tunnel I'd been struggling through for two years. Partly, it was the result of practical considerations – I began to see that there was more choice about what I could do with my life than I had thought. I didn't need to stay where I was – I could get up and take off in any direction I chose. I could earn money and use it to work towards independence and I could become master of my own destiny instead of feeling it depended on so many others. The sight of this approaching independence excited me so much I forgot for the first time in years to ask what was the point. I no longer felt I was marking time in that mournful no-man's land between childhood and maturity – I was out of it. I set my sights on far-off goals – Oxford, a book published, a house of my own, worldwide travel – and in the hard work to attain overcame boredom and discontent.

But more important than economic factors was the growing certainty that I wasn't in some way peculiar – I had begun to find other people like myself with the same attitudes, the same aspirations, people who asked the same questions. I couldn't identify with my long-suffering family but there were plenty of others out there with whom I could. That pointlessness about life that had so worried me now seemed attractive – if everything was pointless then why worry, why not sit back and enjoy it?

Nothing since has ever seemed quite as bleak as that adolescent vision of hopelessness. Many, many times I have had far more cause for despair than I did then, and yet not felt in the least despairing. I don't think I have ever been truly depressed since I was fifteen and I cannot help but think that those years were so very bad partly because I let them be.

The Badness Within Him
SUSAN HILL

A terrible story. To feel guilty about childhood hatred and fantasies is one thing. For no one grows up without hearing, 'That's bad ... What's got into you? ... How can you be so mean?' And almost no one grows up without enduring a summer like the one young Col has, when the shabby sandy house is suddenly a prison, the holidays a boredom of eternity, and the familiar people disgusting enemies.

But to have your lonely illusions of evil confirmed by events – there is the horror. It seems there can be no growing out of this summer for Col.

MONICA DICKENS

*

The night before, he had knelt beside his bed and prayed for a storm, an urgent, hysterical prayer. But even while he prayed he had known that there could be no answer, because of the badness within him, a badness which was living and growing like a cancer. So that he was not surprised to draw back the curtains and see the pale, glittering mist of another hot day. But he was angry. He did not want the sun and the endless stillness and brightness, the hard-edged shadows and the steely gleam of the sea. They came to this place every summer, they had been here, now, since the first of August, and they had one week more left. The sun had shone from the beginning. He wondered how he would bear it.

At the breakfast table, Jess sat opposite to him and her hand kept moving up to rub at the sunburned skin which was peeling off her nose.

'Stop *doing* that.'

Jess looked up slowly. This year, for the first time, Col felt the difference in age between them, he saw that Jess was changing, moving away from him to join the adults. She was almost fourteen.

'What if the skin doesn't grow again? What then? You look awful enough now.'

She did not reply, only considered him for a long time, before returning her attention to the cereal plate. After a moment, her hand went up again to the peeling skin.

Col thought, I hate it here. I hate it. *I hate it.* And he clenched his fist under cover of the table until the fingernails hurt him, digging into his palm. He had suddenly come to hate it, and the emotion frightened him. It was the reason why he had prayed for the storm, to break the pattern of long, hot, still days and waken the others out of their contentment, to change things. Now, everything was as it had always been in the past and he did not want the past, he wanted the future.

But the others were happy here, they slipped into the gentle, lazy routine of summer as their feet slipped into sandals, they never grew bored or angry or irritable, never quarrelled with one another. For days now Col had wanted to quarrel.

How had he ever been able to bear it? And he cast about, in his frustration, for some terrible event, as he felt the misery welling up inside him at the beginning of another day.

I hate it here. He hated the house itself, the chintz curtains and covers bleached by the glare of the sun, and the crunch of sand like sugar spilled in the hall and along the tiled passages, the windows with peeling paint always open on to the garden, and the porch cluttered with sandshoes and buckets and deck-chairs, the muddle and shabbiness of it all.

They all came down to breakfast at different times, and ate slowly and talked of nothing, made no plans, for that was what the holiday was for, a respite from plans and time-tables.

Fay pulled out the high chair and sat her baby down next to Col.

'You can help him with his egg.'

'Do I have to?'

Fay stared at him, shocked that anyone should not find her child desirable.

'Do help, Col, you know the baby can't manage by himself.'

'Col's got a black dog on his shoulder.'

'Shut up.'

'A perfectly enormous, coal black, monster of a dog!'

He kicked out viciously at his sister under the table. Jess began to cry.

'Now, Col, you are to apologize please.' His mother looked paler than ever, exhausted. Fay's baby dug fingers of toast down deeper and deeper into the yolk of egg.

'You hurt me, you hurt me.'

He looked out of the window. The sea was a thin, glistening line. Nothing moved. Today would be the same as yesterday and all the other days – nothing would happen, nothing would change. He felt himself itching beneath his skin.

They had first come here when he was three years old. He remembered how great the distance had seemed as he jumped from rock to rock on the beach, how he had scarcely been able to stretch his leg across and balance. Then, he had stood for minute after minute feeling the damp ribs of sand under his feet. He had been enchanted with everything. He and Jess had collected buckets full of sea creatures from the rock pools and put them into a glass aquarium in the scullery, though always the starfish and anemones and limpets died after a few, captive days. They had taken jam jars up on to West Cliff and walked along, at the hottest part of the day, looking for chrysalis on the grass stalks. The salt had dried in white tide marks around their brown legs, and Col had reached down and rubbed some off with his finger and then licked it. In the sun lounge the moths and butterflies had swollen and cracked open their frail, papery coverings and crept out like babies from the womb, and he and Jess had sat up half the night by the light of moon or candle, watching them.

And so it had been every year and often, in winter or windy spring in London, he remembered it all, the smell of the sunlit house and the feeling of the warm sea lapping against his thighs and the line of damp woollen bathing shorts outside the open back door. It was another world, but it was still there, and when every summer came they would return to it, things would be the same.

Yet now, he wanted to do some violence in this house, he wanted an end to everything. He was afraid of himself.

'Col's got a black dog on his shoulder!'

So he left them and went for a walk on his own, over the track beside the gorse bushes and up on to the coarse grass of the sheep field behind West Cliff. The mist was rolling away, the sea was white-gold at the edges, creaming back. On the far side of the field there were poppies.

He lay down and pressed his face and hands into the warm turf until he could smell the soil beneath and, gradually, he felt the warmth of the sun on his back and it soothed him.

In the house, his mother and sisters left the breakfast table and wandered upstairs to find towels and sunhats and books, content that this day should be the same as all the other days, wanting the summer to last. And later, his father would join them for the week-end, coming down on the train from London, he would discard the blue city suit and emerge, hairy and thickly fleshed, to lie on a rug and snore and play with Fay's baby, rounding off the family circle.

By eleven it was hotter than it had been all summer, the dust rose in soft clouds when a car passed down the lane to the village, and did not settle again, and the leaves of the hedges were mottled and dark, the birds went quiet. Col felt his own anger like a pain tightening around his head. He went up to the house and lay on his bed trying to read, but the room was airless and the sunlight fell in a straight, hard beam across his bed and on to the printed page, making his eyes hurt.

When he was younger he had liked this room, he had some-times dreamed of it when he was in London. He had collected shells and small pebbles and laid them out in careful piles, and hung up a bladder-wrack on a nail by the open window, had brought books from home about fossils and shipwrecks and propped them on top of the painted wooden chest. But now it felt too small, it stifled him, it was a childish room, a pale, dead room in which nothing ever happened and nothing would change.

After a while he heard his father's taxi come up the drive.

'Col, do watch what you're doing near the baby, you'll get sand in his eyes.'

'Col, if you want to play this game with us, do, but other-wise go away, if you can't keep still, you're just spoiling it.'

'Col, why don't you build a sandcastle or something?'

He stood looking down at them all, at his mother and Fay playing cards in the shade of the green parasol, and his father lying on his back, his bare, black-haired chest shiny with oil and his nostrils flaring in and out as he breathed, at Jess, who had begun to build the sandcastle for the baby, instead of him. She had her hair tied back in bunches and the freckles had come out even more thickly across her cheekbones, she might have been eleven years old. But she was almost four-teen, she had gone away from him.

'Col, don't kick the sand like that, it's flying everywhere. Why don't you go and have a swim? Why can't you find something to do? I do so dislike you just hovering over us like that.'

Jess had filled a small bucket with water from the rock pool, and now she bent down and began to pour it carefully into the moat. It splashed on to her bare feet and she wriggled her toes. Fay's baby bounced up and down with interest and pleasure in the stream of water and the crenellated golden castle.

Col kicked again more forcefully. The clods of sand hit the tower of the castle sideways, and, as it fell, crumbled the edges off the other towers and broke open the surrounding wall, so that everything toppled into the moat, clouding the water.

Jess got to her feet, scarlet in the face, ready to hit out at him.

'I hate you. *I hate you.*'

'Jess . . .'

'He wants to spoil everything, look at him, he doesn't want anyone else to enjoy themselves, he just wants to sulk and . . . I hate him.'

Col thought, I am filled with evil, there is no hope for me. For he felt himself completely taken over by the badness within him.

'*I hate you.*'

He turned away from his sister's wild face and her mouth which opened and shut over and over again to shout her rejection of him, turned away from them all and began to walk towards the caves at the far side of the cove. Above them were the cliffs.

Three-quarters of the way up there was a ledge around which the gannets and kittiwakes nested. He had never climbed up as high as this before. There were tussocks of grass, dried and bleached bone-pale by the sea winds, and he clung on to them and to the bumps of chalky rock. Flowers grew, pale wild scabious and cliff buttercups, and when he rested, he touched his face to them. Above his head, the sky was enamel blue. The sea birds watched him with eyes like beads. As he climbed higher, the wash of the sea and the voices of those on the beach receded. When he reached the ledge, he got his breath and then sat down cautiously, legs dangling over the edge. There was just enough room for him. The surface of the cliff was hot on his back. He was not at all afraid.

His family were like insects down on the sand, little shapes of colour dotted about at random. Jess was a pink shape, the parasol was bottle-glass green, Fay and Fay's baby were yellow. For most of the time they were still, but once they all clustered around the parasol to look at something and then broke away again, so that it was like a dance. The other people on the beach were quite separate, each family kept itself to itself. Out beyond the curve of the cliff the beach lay like a ribbon bounded by the tide, which did not reach as far as the cove except in the storms of winter. They had never been here during the winter.

When Col opened his eyes again his head swam for a moment. Everything was the same. The sky was thin and clear. The sun shone. If he had gone to sleep he might have tipped over and fallen forwards. The thought did not frighten him.

But all was not the same, for now he saw his father had left the family group and was padding down towards the sea. The black hairs curled up the backs of his legs and the soles of his feet were brownish pink as they turned up one after the other.

Col said, do I like my father? And thought about it. And did not know.

Fay's baby was crawling after him, its lemon-coloured behind stuck up in the air.

Now, Col half-closed his eyes, so that air and sea and sand shimmered, merging together.

Now, he felt rested, no longer angry, he felt above it all.

Now, he opened his eyes again and saw his father striding

into the water, until it reached up to his chest: then he flopped on to his belly and floated for a moment, before beginning to swim.

Col thought, perhaps I am ill and *that* is the badness within me.

But if he had changed, the others had changed too. Since Fay had married and had the baby and gone to live in Berkshire, she was different, she fussed more, was concerned with the details of things, she spoke to them all a trifle impatiently. And his mother was so languid. And Jess – Jess did not want his company.

Now he saw his father's dark head bobbing up and down quite a long way out to sea, but as he watched, sitting on the high cliff ledge in the sun, the bobbing stopped – began again – an arm came up and waved, though as if it were uncertain of its direction.

Col waved back.

The sun was burning the top of his head.

Fay and Fay's baby and Jess had moved in around the parasol again, their heads were bent together. Col thought, we will never be the same with one another, the ties of blood make no difference, we are separate people now. And then he felt afraid of such truth. Father's waving stopped abruptly, he bobbed and disappeared, bobbed up again.

The sea was still as glass.

Col saw that his father was drowning.

In the end, a man from the other side of the beach went running down to the water's edge and another to where the family were grouped around the parasol. Col looked at the cliff, falling away at his feet. He closed his eyes and turned around slowly and then got down on his hands and knees and began to feel for a foothold, though not daring to look. His head was hot and throbbing.

By the time he reached the bottom, they were bringing his

father's body. Col stood in the shadow of the cliff and shivered and smelled the dank, cave smell behind him. His mother and Fay and Jess stood in a line, very erect, like Royalty at the cenotaph, and in Fay's arms the baby was still as a doll.

Everyone else kept away, though Col could see that they made half-gestures, raised an arm or turned a head, occasionally took an uncertain step forward, before retreating again.

Eventually he wondered if they had forgotten about him. The men dripped water off their arms and shoulders as they walked and the sea ran off the body, too, in a thin, steady stream.

Nobody spoke to him about the cliff climb. People only spoke of baths and hot drinks and telephone messages, scarcely looking at one another as they did so, and the house was full of strangers moving from room to room.

In bed, he lay stiffly under the tight sheets and looked towards the window where the moon shone. He thought, it is my fault. I prayed for some terrible happening and the badness within me made it come about. I am punished. For this was a change greater than any he could have imagined.

When he slept he dreamed of drowning, and woke early, just at dawn. Outside the window, a dove grey mist muffled everything. He felt the cold linoleum under his feet and the dampness in his nostrils. When he reached the bottom of the stairs he saw at once that the door of the sun parlour was closed. He stood for a moment outside, listening to the creaking of the house, imagining all of them in their beds, his mother lying alone. He was afraid. He turned the brass doorknob and went slowly in.

There were windows on three sides of the room, long and uncurtained, with a view of the sea, but now there was only the fog pressing up against the panes, the curious stillness. The floor was polished and partly covered with rush matting and in the ruts of this the sand of all the summer past had gathered and lay, soft and gritty, the room smelled of sea-weed. On the walls, the sepia photographs of his great-grandfather the Captain, and his naval friends and their ships. He had always liked this room. When he was small, he had sat here with his mother on warm, August evenings, drinking his mug of milk, and the smell of stocks came into them from the open windows. The deckchairs had always been in a row outside on the terrace, empty at the end of the day. He stepped forward.

They had put his father's body on the trestle, dressed in a shirt and covered with a sheet and a rug. His head was bare and lay on a cushion, and the hands, with the black hair over their backs, were folded together. Now, he was not afraid. His father's skin was oddly pale and shiny. He stared, trying to feel some sense of loss and sorrow. He had watched his father drown, though for a long time he had not believed it, the water had been so entirely calm. Later, he had heard them talking of a heart attack, and then he had understood better why this strong barrel of a man, down that day from the City, should have been so suddenly sinking, sinking.

The fog horn sounded outside. Then, he knew that the change had come, knew that the long, hot summer was at an end, and that his childhood had ended too, that they would never come to this house again. He knew, finally, the power of the badness within him and because of that, standing close to his father's body, he wept.

Bubblefoot
LEON GARFIELD

An allegory of loneliness, set nowhere in time, but with a kind of
Dickensian flavour which may make you visualize it happening
in eighteenth-century London, where a child could starve and rot
unnoticed.

It is a version of the rewarding formula: the camel can't get
through the needle's eye, the outcast is the chosen one. This never
seems quite true in our shakily democratic world of continuing
privilege and poverty, so we make it happen in stories and fables.
This is the way it *ought* to be. 'The least of these my brethren'
shall see God.

MONICA DICKENS

*

Every night, from about two hours after dark till the first
thread of dawn, Bubblefoot is on duty in Covent Garden,
between the Marquis of Anglesey and the Nag's Head.

'Bubblefoot, sir! 'ere's Bubblefoot!'

He is short, of an earthy complexion, and gives off a smell
out of all proportion to his size. He might be eight years old;
he might be nine. Ten would be stretching it ... but why
not?

'Bubblefoot at yer service, sir!'

His curious name is on account of a mysterious deformity
that causes him to hop and squelch as he goes along; as if he
has an egg in his boot, and a bad one at that! Nobody knows
where he's come from; his beginnings, like the rest of him, are
wrapped in a grubby mystery.

'Over 'ere, sir! Look dahn a bit an ye'll 'ave us in yer
peepers!'

My God! Though everybody must have had a mother, it's impossible to think of Bubblefoot's having had one. Much easier to suppose that he's a spontaneous happening straight out of the soil of the night. He couldn't have *grown* that way!

'Now you got us, sir; fair 'n' square! Jus' yer stand steady an' leave it to Bubblefoot!'

He earns his bread by looking after drunken gentlemen and taking them home; which he does with an affability and importance worthy of an archbishop.

'Nar tell us where yer lives, sir, an' us'll see yer safe 'n' sound!'

Nobody has ever appointed him to this office, but somehow he's come to regard it as a solemn duty and so necessary that the world could not get on very well without him. Even when grievously sick (Bubblefoot often has coughs, colds, cramps and retchings – and, very likely, distemper and the mange, as his state is not much different from that of a stray cat or dog), he turns up.

'Us is all right, sir. Nuffink ketching.'

Bilious wraith or sneezing hobgoblin – as if come to lead the drunkard mischievously into briar, pond or ditch – he lifts a twiggy finger in salute. Sneezes thrice, wipes his snout on his sleeve (which glistens as if with dew), and shows an encouraging tooth.

'Us'll see yer 'ome, sir. That's what we're 'ere fer.'

So where's he gone now? Over in a corner to spit. He has a chill on him that would have laid up an alderman for a week; but duty must be done.

' 'ere we are agin, sir! Where to, sir? Didn't quite ketch the name? Ah! Golden Shquare. Knows it like the back of our 'and!'

Off he goes: bubble – hop! . . . bubble – hop! through fog, rain and that curious, syrupy gloom, shot through with bending windows and double lamps, that the drunkard knows so well.

'Jes' foller us, sir,' he urges, leading his gent between treacherous posts and along dark alleys where snakes lie coiled and spitting in deep down, dark down pits. 'Us'll 'ave yer safe 'n' sound!'

He always speaks of himself in the plural, as if he understands that, in a drunkard's eyes, he's most likely more than one.

'Watch out, sir! Watch out! That's where them 'orrible creechers come crawlin' out o' the wall!'

He knows it all: the burning serpents, the green spiders with ladies' hands, and the huge pink rats that gnaw away at the dome of St Paul's, as if it was a cake with a sugar cross. He's never seen them himself, but he's been told about them by gentlemen who'd sooner split their tongues than tell him lies.

So it's gospel truth, all of it; and it's the only truth he knows. As nobody sober has ever said more to him than, 'Ugh!' or, 'Whew!' he learns from the only conversations he has.

'Ellyfunts, sir? Yeller ellyfunts? An' what's them when they're at 'ome? Ah! 'orrible, 'orrible!' says Bubblefoot, stocking up his mind. 'Not much furder now, sir. Nearly 'ome. Jus' dahn there, ain't it?'

It isn't, of course; but no matter, Bubblefoot isn't lost. Like he says, he knows the town like the back of his hand; only – only he doesn't know the *names* of places. So where's Golden Square? Easy. Through Bubblefoot's mind has passed – in a series of window, railing and doorknocker flashes – all the lanes, alleys and courts in creation; and he's picked on one of them as being very likely.

''ere we are, sir! Golden Shquare.' (Which it isn't.) ' 'ome. That'll be a penny, sir. Fer Bubblefoot dahn 'ere. It's our fee.'

Then off he hops, stinking the night out, and leaving his gent to come to his senses in what might as well be the other side of the moon.

He doesn't do it on purpose, of course; in fact, if all the gentlemen he's led astray were laid end to end as a reproach before him, he'd be absolutely astonished!

'Garn!' he'd say. 'Get away wiv' yer!'

There's no malice in Bubblefoot. He's always done his duty with the best will in the world. It's just that all he knows is what drunkards have told him, so his best will, like his world, is topsy-turvy.

So back he goes to the Garden, late as a dead owl. Already his eyes look as if worms have been sleeping in them, and his chest aches like a tooth. Even the sky seems to have caught his cold, for it's sneezed all over with stars.

Shadows cluster, as if frightened of the dark; monsters lurk but dare not show themselves. It is a weird, hot-and-cold night, stinging with pins and needles and full of torn curtains that brush the eyes. Bubblefoot is weary unto death, and would like to go to sleep . . . for a long, long time.

He sits himself down and considers the gruesome world that lies between sleeping and sleeping . . . then he gets up again, with a sniff and a wipe of his snout.

'Bubblefoot 'ere, sir. 'ere's Bubblefoot.'

Just his luck. A last gent has come floating out of somewhere on wings of wine. A very torn and bleeding gent, who looks like he's had more than words with some landlord before being booted out. A lean and whiskery gent, whose eyes keep rolling round and round, as if they're a bad fit.

'A fightin' gent,' thinks Bubblefoot gloomily. 'Them's worse'n the screamin' ones, worse'n the cryin' ones, worse'n the sick 'uns . . . because you never gets paid.' But duty must be done.

'Over 'ere, sir,' says Bubblefoot. 'Look dahn a bit an' ye'll 'ave us in yer peepers.'

The ragged one looks and looks.

'Now you got us, sir . . . jes' keep steady an' yer got us fair 'n' square.'

Wild eyes stop rolling. They grow huge and Bubblefoot suddenly fears they'll fall right out and leave behind empty dishes of bone . . . like the remains of a supper of worms.

'Jes' tell us where yer lives, sir, an' Bubblefoot'll see yer 'ome.'

'Which one of you?' says the gent, looking hard. 'I can see . . . thousands!'

Bubblefoot nods. He understands. Lifts a twiggy finger, archbishop-like.

'Jes' foller all of us, sir. Foller the crahd an' us'll see yer safe 'n' sound!'

But this time Bubblefoot has got a right one, who doesn't know where he lives; or won't say.

'*You* follow ME!' he says, and folds his way round a post; several times. He stops; looks everywhere and ends by frowning up at the stars as if, the last time he noticed them, they were under foot. He sighs, and Bubblefoot is enveloped in wine-rich air, thick enough to walk on.

Bubblefoot feels sick and dizzy and the night runs ice-cold fingers up his back. He sneezes violently. The gent scowls and wipes the backs of his bleeding hands on his whiskers, very genteel like.

'Us is all right, sir,' says Bubblefoot, apologetically. 'Nuffink ketching.'

He looks up at the frowning houses as if in confirmation. One by one the chimney tops seem to slide away. Don't want what you've got, Bubblefoot. The cobbles hasten off into shadow. Don't want what you've got, Bubblefoot. Even the stars turn away their bright faces. Don't want what you've got, Bubblefoot . . .

'No,' says the bleeding gent. 'Not catching.'

But there's something about the way he says it that makes Bubblefoot wish that, whatever it is he's got, *was* catching; for even this last gent, ragged as he is, seems to be backing away from him.

'Where are yer orf to, sir?' (More of a wail than an inquiry.)

'Follow me . . .

'Us'll take yer,' says Bubblefoot, obstinately. 'Jus' tell us where.'

No good. Bubblefoot's never had such an awkward, boozy, battered gent in all his born nights. Look at him now! Lifting up a finger as if to see which way the wind's blowing! He's off.

'Follow me . . .'

First he goes along a thin old street, bending forward as if it's uphill when it's down; and then he starts staggering as if he's carrying something heavy enough to break his back.

'Watch out, mister!' calls Bubblefoot, hopping after. 'That's where them 'orrible creechers come crawlin' out o' the wall!'

'What creatures?' He leans against a doorway to rest.

Bubblefoot limps up to tell him (as if he didn't know!). He tells him of the snakes and spiders, the great pink rats and all the other terrible phantoms that inhabit the vineyards of the night. He tells him of households falling, falling in streamers of blood and tears; of bricks that weep and hearts built so strong and high that they shut out the light. Proudly he tells him everything he knows about; for it's not often that Bubblefoot has a chance to talk.

'And where are they now?' asks the gent abruptly, as if coming out of a deep reverie. He pushes himself upright and glares ferociously, with wine-bright eyes.

' 'e's goin' to fight,' thinks Bubblefoot wearily. ' 'e's goin' to bash in a winder or sumfink. Them fightin' gents is always the worst!'

'I'll smash them!' shouts the ragged one, making fists as wild as fireflies. 'I'll crash them! I'll blow them all to Kingdom come!'

Then, to Bubblefoot's further discomfiture, he launches

himself into the middle of the street and begins a war-dance of fists, boots, elbows and knees.

'I'll smash them! I'll crash them! Like that! Like that! And another one! Begone! Begone, you foul things!'

Now down the street he capers, whirling round corners, swinging on posts. Sometimes, with arms outstretched, like a great tattered bird, he swoops, bending from side to side; hunting ... chasing ... pouncing! Then up the sides of the houses where the green spiders crawl ...

'Begone! Begone, I say!'

'Oh mister,' thinks Bubblefoot, hopping and limping in and out of the way. 'Yer've 'ad a skinful tonight, all right!'

Suddenly he stops his antics. He turns about and presents to Bubblefoot the most enormous smile.

('A joker!' thinks Bubblefoot. 'Worse, even, than them fightin' gents!')

'We've won!' says the joker. 'Now for a victory dance!'

'But us is poorly mister. Dreadful poorly ...'

'Dance! Dance!'

'But us 'as a disability, mister. Us 'as a rotten foot!'

'Dance! Dance!'

Then before Bubblefoot can hop away, he finds himself caught and whirled up and around. ('Them dancin' gents is worst of all!')

Round and round, down streets and alleys, through courts and across solemn squares; windows come out on stalks and the houses turn over and stand on their chimneys – which are toes. Stars and cobbles ... lamps and eyes ... and a roaring in Bubblefoot's ears as breath of wine beats round him like a billowing sea. No time to limp; nothing to limp on ... Bubblefoot prances on air.

'Oh mister!' he wails breathlessly. 'Tell us where's yer 'ome?'

'Oh I'll tell you – I'll tell you –' cries out the dancing gent, into Bubblefoot's passing ear. 'I'll tell you –' and he tells him

jokes and stories ... sings him snatches of song ... and he's
aways laughing ... laughing fit to burst.

'Oh mister, mister!'

'It's something catching, Bubblefoot! Catch it – catch it
while you can!'

It's the laughter that's catching and, try as he might to
stop himself, Bubblefoot begins to laugh. He laughs and
coughs and laughs and sneezes, and once he laughs bright
blood.

The dance stops. The houses put up their chimneys and
smooth down their doors and bricks. The cobbles go back into
the street and the stars return to the sky. Bubblefoot leans
panting against a wall; and the dancer says:

'It's time to go home, now.'

'Where, mister? Where is it?'

There's a door, tall enough for a horse to go through without nodding.

'Here,' says the ragged one; and pushes it open. 'Will you
come in?'

Bubblefoot ponders. Such a thing has never happened to
him before.

'Nar,' he says at length. 'Yore pa would 'ave us out
sooner'n spit!'

'We'll be quiet. Quiet as mice.'

'Nar!' says Bubblefoot. 'Yore ma'd smell us a mile off!'

The ragged one chuckles and takes Bubblefoot by the hand.
'It's my house, you know.'

All is dim within. Huge pale walls vanish up, up into a
gloom. Many carved seats, some with grinning faces. And far
off, a great table, set with golden candlesticks and a white
cloth. It is more splendid, even, than the Nag's Head.

'Sit here, Bubblefoot. Rest.'

'Where are yer goin', mister?'

'To look for my pa.'

'Let me come wiv' yer, mister?'

The ragged one pauses . . . and shakes his head.

'Wait for me here.'

'Will yer be long gone?'

'I'll be back . . . I'll be back . . .'

He goes, soft as a dream, and Bubblefoot is left alone. Slowly his eyes close . . . and he sleeps.

Morning. A priest, oiled and seasoned with grace, Geneva bands, like a folded angel, trapped under his chin, enters his church. He pauses. A bad, bad smell. He frowns, wrinkles his nose and begins to search for a dead cat, a dead dog, a dead anything.

Presently he finds a small earthy person, stinking unmentionably, dead in his best pew. Dead . . . or asleep? He goes away and comes back with a long stick. He pokes the hopeless bundle of rags.

An eye opens, like a jewel in the gutter.

'Oi!' says Bubblefoot; and sneezes.

'What are you doing here?' demands the priest, warding off infection.

'Waitn' fer our gent,' says Bubblefoot, wiping his nose between his convenient knees.

'What gent?' (Looks to see if the candlesticks have gone.)

' 'im what brung us 'ere, of course! Said 'e'd be back.'

(Thieves in the night! Is the roof still on?)

'Get out of here!'

'But 'e told us to wait fer 'im!'

'Who told you to wait?'

The earthy person looks everywhere. Ferrety eyes sneak into corners, round the pews, up the altar . . . Suddenly they widen, and into them comes a look of horror and grief! Such a look! There's no mistaking it and the priest feels a chill of dread.

'That's 'im!' screeches the child, lifting a horrible finger. 'Up there! Wotcher do it fer? Wotcher kill 'im fer, mister?

An' wiv' them 'orrible nails! You done 'im in, mister! An' in 'is own 'ouse! Wotcher 'ang 'im up fer ... like butcher's meat? 'e were so 'appy last night! 'e was dancin' an' singin' an tellin' us jokes!'

Then Bubblefoot sets up an unearthly howl of despair as he stares up at his gent, crowned with thorns and hanging on a cross.

No! He's not lying! thinks the priest, bewildered out of his gracious senses. He's too ignorant to tell lies!

'What – what did he say to you, child?'

' 'e said 'e was goin' to find 'is pa. I arst to go wiv' 'im, but 'e said to wait. 'e promised 'e'd be back.'

Why, why didn't you take him, thinks the priest. Why did you leave him to wait for you in this harsh world?

Bubblefoot wipes his eyes clean. Suddenly he grins.

'Now I sees it! Yore 'avin' me on, mister! That ain't 'im at all! Very like 'im, though. Only 'e was laughin' ...'

He was laughing? thinks the priest, looking up at the man of sorrows, hanging in the rich church. How strange, he thinks, how very strange for rags to be so handsomely gilded, nails to be made of silver, and thorns of fine-spun gold? How odd for blood to be painted, when every man bleeds for nothing and paint costs so dear! What a topsy-turvy world it is – a drunkards' world!

As he thinks and thinks, it seems as if the centuries roll by, like an old yellow varnish; and the sky comes through, bright and clear.

'Child,' says he, taking hold of Bubblefoot's dreadful hand. 'I, too, am waiting for – for our gent. So we'll wait together, shall we? you and me in his house.'

'Can't stay long,' says Bubblefoot, archbishop-like. 'Got our duty to do.'

'And what's that?'

'I shows gents the way 'ome.'

The priest looks up at the cross – and suddenly he laughs;

he laughs until the tears leap out of his eyes. 'So,' thinks he. 'That's why you didn't take him! That's why you left him . . . to wait!' His hand tightens on Bubblefoot's as if he'll never let him go.

'Come, child,' says he. 'Let's make our gent's house ready for when he comes again!'

'Will it take long?'

'All our lives.'

'Well,' says Bubblefoot, 'seein' as 'ow 'e told us to wait . . . Where do we begin, mister?'

A Very Long Way from Anywhere Else

URSULA LE GUIN

A situation, played too often in too many families which seem close, but are snakepits of frustration just below the surface.

Dad has bought Owen a car. He doesn't want it because that would make him a 'normal car-loving American teenager'. But if he has no car, he can't drive himself to the state college his mother has picked. He would rather die than go there. 'Look, son, it's great to dream of Princeton, but we can't afford it.'

Screaming silently, son slams out of house.

He's got to come back, having nowhere else to live, but they'd all be better apart. Once families have broken free of the claustrophobic war of upbringing, it's easier to come together again as friends. The salvation is Natalie, who plays the violin and who *listens*.

This tense, wincingly true story is a reminder of the thing most likely to help: someone to talk to. *What can I do? What can I say? How can I handle this?* We panic, when someone comes to us in distress. Try this: Shut up and listen.

MONICA DICKENS

*

The reason I have reported that conversation on the bus with Natalie Field so exactly is that it was an unimportant conversation that was extremely important to me. And that's important, that something unimportant can be so important.

I guess I tend to think that important events should be solemn, and very grand, with muted violins playing in the background. It's hard to realize that the really important things are just normal little happenings and decisions, and when they turn on the background music and the spotlights and the uniforms, nothing important is going to happen at all.

What stuck in my head after that conversation was just one word, the most commonplace, meaningless word. It wasn't the way she looked, or the way she looked at me, or my acting like a clown and making her laugh, or it was all that, but all sort of compressed into one word, 'Yeah,' the way she said it. Firmly, certainly. Yeah, that's what you're going to do. It was like a rock. Whenever I looked into my head there was this rock.

And I needed a rock. Something to hold on to, to stand on. Something solid. Because everything was going soft, turning into mush, into marsh, into fog. Fog closing in on all sides. I didn't know where I was at all.

It was really getting bad. It had been coming for a while, for a long while I guess, but it was the car that really brought it on.

You see, in giving me that car my father was saying, 'This is what I want you to be. A normal car-loving American teenager.' And by giving it to me he had made it impossible for me to say what I wanted to say, which was that I had finally realized that that's what I wasn't, and was never going to be, and I needed help finding out what I was instead. But to say that, now, I had to say, 'Take your present back. I don't want it!' And I couldn't. He'd put his heart into that gift. It was the best he could possibly give me. And was I supposed to say, 'Take yourself back, Dad, I don't want you'?

I think my mother understood all that, but in a way that wasn't any use to me. My mother was and is a good wife. Being a good wife and mother is the important thing in her life. And she is a good wife and mother. She never lets my father down. She nags him about some things, of course, but she never sneers at him or cuts him down, the way I've heard women do to their husbands; in all the big things she backs him up – what he does is right. And she keeps the house clean and cooks really well and makes extra stuff like biscuits and muesli and when you want a clean shirt there is one and when Muscular Dystrophy or some other charity organization wants a co-ordinator or a door-to-door collector she does it. And if you think all that, running even a small family and house so that things are decent and peaceful, is a small job, maybe you ought to try it for a year or two. She works hard and uses her head at it. But the trouble is, she's afraid of doing anything else, of being anything else. Not afraid for herself, I think, but afraid that if she did anything except look after us, she'd be letting us down – letting the side down, not being a good wife and mother. She feels she's got to be always there. She can't even take off the time it takes to read a novel. I think she doesn't read novels because if she got really interested in one, absorbed, then she'd be somewhere else, by herself: she wouldn't be with us. And that's wrong, to her. So all she ever reads are some magazines about food and interior decorating and one about extremely expensive holiday travel to places she doesn't want to go to. My father watches a lot of TV but she never pays much attention to it; she may be sitting there with him in the living room, but she's sewing or doing crewelwork or figuring out household stuff or working on Muscular Dystrophy lists. Ready to get up and do what needs doing.

She didn't spoil me, more than an only kid always gets spoiled by being the centre of attention. She used to try to keep me from reading so much, but she sort of gave up when I was twelve or thirteen. As far back as I can remember, I had to keep my room straight and do garden jobs. I do the lawn and carry out rubbish and so on. Male jobs only, of course. I never learned how to work the washing machine till the time she had to have an operation and couldn't climb stairs for two weeks. I don't think my father knows how to work it yet. That's woman's work. It's funny, really, because he's nuts about machines. All our appliances have to have about twelve different cycles and all possible attachments. If he ever bought the plain ordinary model of anything he'd feel he wasn't treating her right. But if they're household work machines, she runs them. And when they break down, she calls the repairman. My father doesn't like to hear about things breaking down.

That's why I couldn't say anything about the car. Because it had really broken me down. It just was the end, the last stop. I had to get off. But there wasn't anything outside the bus but rain and fog and me jumping up and down doing an ape act and nobody looking or hearing.

I came in from the bus stop that day. My mother was in the kitchen blending something in the blender. She yelled something over the scream of the machine but I couldn't hear what. I went up to my room and dropped my knapsack and took off my coat with the wet collar and stood there. The rain was whacking on the roof. I said, 'I am an intellectual. I am an intellectual. I am an intellectual. And the rest of you can go to hell!'

I heard my voice and it sounded unbelievably feeble. Big deal! So I was an intellectual, and what else is new? That's when the fog closed in completely. And that's when I found the rock. It was actually like that, as if my hand closed around a solid, round rock. The girl on the bus saying, 'Yeah,' in that solid, round voice. Yeah: good. So go ahead and be what you are.

So when I had rubbed some of the rain out of my hair with a towel, I sat down at my desk and started to reread Ornstein's *The Psychology of Consciousness*. Because something like that, thinking about how we actually think, how our heads work, is what I would like to do.

But it didn't last. I dropped the rock. At dinner my father got going about how you break in a new car. You should drive it at moderate speeds every day, and going to and from school would be perfect for it. 'If you want me to take it to work for a week or so of course I'll be glad to,' he said. 'It's not good for a new car just to sit there.'

'OK,' I said, ' you do that.'

That blew it. His face got tight. 'If you didn't want the car, you might have told me.'

'You never asked me if I wanted a car.'

His face got tighter, like a clenched fist. He said, 'It's been driven very little. I suppose the dealer might take it back. Not for the full cost, of course. They couldn't resell it as new.'

'Oh rubbish, what a notion,' my mother said. 'How is Owen to get back and forth from State every day next year without a car of his own? It would take him an hour each way on the bus. For goodness sake, Jim, don't expect him to start living in the car right off! If you want to drive it to the office, do. But it'll get plenty of use next year!'

That was fine. My mother is a highly intelligent person. She had just given my father his first practical reason for giving me a car – his excuse, his justification. State University is right on the other edge of our city, about ten miles from where we live. I would certainly need a car to get to classes there next year. The only trouble was that State was not where I wanted to go to college.

But if I brought that up, if I said, 'What if I go away to college?' I'd have blown it again. We'd have had two quarrels going instead of one. Because it was my mother who was dead set on my going to State. And I do mean dead set. She'd gone there, she met Dad there, she quit before she'd finished the course to get married. She knew State. It was safe. The places I wanted to go weren't safe. They were far away, and she didn't understand what went on at them; they were full of communists and radicals and intellectuals.

I had applied to MIT, Cal Tech., and Princeton, as well as State. My father had filled out the scholarship applications and paid the application fees. The forms were incredible, all in quadruplicate, but being a chartered accountant, he rather enjoyed filling them out clearly and honestly, and he didn't mind the fees because I think he took some pride in my shooting for the moon. I expect he mentioned to his friends at the office that his son was applying to Princeton. That was something to be proud of, especially if I didn't actually go there. But he said nothing about it to my mother, as far as I know, and she said nothing about it to either of us. If we wanted to throw away ninety dollars on fees, all right. But her son was going to State.

And she had a practical reason. A very sound one. They could afford to send me there.

I didn't say anything. I couldn't. My jaws locked. I couldn't swallow the piece of pot roast I'd been working on, either. It just lay there in my mouth, a fibrous sort of lump. I couldn't chew it. I worked it over to one side, and drank some milk around it, and after a long time I managed to chew it and swallow it. After a longer time dinner was over. I went up to do homework.

It was no good. Why should I study? What for? I could get to State without studying. I could probably get right through State without studying. I could probably go on and become an accountant or a tax auditor or a maths teacher and be respectable and successful and get married and have a family and buy a house and get old and die without ever studying, without ever thinking at all. Why not? A lot of other people did. You think you're so special, Griffiths.

I couldn't stand the sight of any of the books in my room, I hated them. I went downstairs and said, 'Going out for a drive,' around the ghost of that piece of beef that still seemed to be in my mouth, and I went out and got into the new car. I had left the keys in it, Sunday. Even Dad hadn't noticed. It could have been stolen any time during the last two days. If only it had been. I started it up and drove very slowly down the street. Breaking it in.

At the end of the block I passed the Fields' house.

OK, now I know I was sick – really sick, a little past the breaking point – that night, because of what I did. I did what any normal car-loving American teenager would do if he'd met a girl he liked. I stopped and backed and parked in front of the Fields' and went up to the front door and knocked and said to Mrs Field, 'Is Natalie here?'

'She's practising.'

'Can I see her for a minute?'

'I'll ask her.'

Mrs Field was a good-looking woman, older than my parents. She had the same severe expression Natalie had, but she was handsomer. Maybe Natalie would be that handsome at fifty. Kind of worn and polished like a piece of granite in a creek. Mrs Field wasn't friendly or unfriendly, welcoming or off-putting. She was calm. She just stated the facts. She stood aside – it was still raining – and let me into the hall; didn't ask me in any farther; went upstairs. As she went, I heard Natalie practising. It must be a violin, I thought. A tremendous noise, even though the Fields' house was bigger than ours and older with thicker walls. A big, sweet, hard, rushing noise, rushing down the scales like a creek over rocks, bright and fierce and then it stopped. I'd stopped it.

I heard Mrs Field upstairs say, 'It's the Griffiths boy.' She knew us mainly because Mother had hooked her last spring for a charity appeal, and she'd been at our house for the planning meeting.

Natalie came downstairs. She was frowning and her hair was all messed up. 'Oh hi, Owen,' she said from a distance roughly equivalent to the orbit of Neptune.

'I'm sorry I stopped you practising,' I said.

'That's all right. What's on your mind?'

I had been going to ask her if she'd like to go for a drive in my new car, but I couldn't. I said, 'I don't know.'

And the ghost of the piece of pot roast came back and filled my entire mouth.

She looked at me, and after this long, horrible silence she said, 'Is something wrong?'

I nodded.

'Are you sick?'

I shook my head. Shaking it seemed to clear it a bit. I said, 'I'm upset. It's something to do with my parents. And stuff. It's not terminal. But I. But I wanted to talk. But I. But I can't.'

She was kind of floored. She said, 'Would you like a glass of milk?'

'I've just eaten dinner.'

'Camomile tea,' she said.

'Peter Rabbit,' I said.

'Come on in.'

'I don't want to interrupt you. Listen. Can I sit and listen to you practise? Would it bother you a lot?'

She hesitated, and then she said, 'No. You want to? It's dull.'

We went to the kitchen, and she poured me a cup of extremely weird tea, and then we went upstairs to this room. What a room! All the walls in the Fields' house were dark, and it all looked kind of bare, kind of calm and severe like Mrs Field, but this room was the barest. It had in it one Oriental rug worn down to the warp or whatever you call it so you could hardly see what colours it had been, and one grand piano, three music stands, and a chair. There were some stacks of music under the windows. I sat down on the rug. 'You can sit in the chair,' she said, 'I stand up to practise.'

'I'm fine here.'

'OK,' she said. 'This is some Bach. I have to cut an audition tape next week.' And she picked up her fiddle off the piano and injected it under her jaw in that peculiar way violinists do – only I figured out from the size that this one was a viola not a violin – and rubbed her bow with rosin and stared at the music on the music stand and started playing.

It wasn't your standard concert performance. For one thing the room was so high and bare that it made the noise loud, hard, so that it sort of rang in your bones (she said afterwards it was a perfect room for practising because she could hear all her mistakes). And she made faces and muttered a lot. And she would play the same bit over and over and over. That crashing run she'd been doing when I came in, she must have done it ten or fifteen times, sometimes going on from it, but coming back to it again, starting over. And every time it was slightly different. Until finally it came out the same twice in a row. She'd got it right. Then she went on. Then when she played the whole movement over, that part sounded the same the third time in a row. Right. Yeah.

It had never occurred to me before that music and thinking are so much alike. In fact you could say music is another way of thinking, or maybe thinking is another kind of music.

They talk about the patience scientists have to have, and how scientific work is 99 per cent drudgery and repetition and neatness and making perfectly sure. And it is. I had a very good bio teacher last year, Miss Capswell, and she and I did some lab work after school in spring term. We were working with bacteria. It was exactly the same thing Natalie was doing with the viola. Everything had to be right. You didn't know for sure what was going to happen when you finally did get it all right: you had to get it right to find out. Miss Capswell and I were trying to confirm an experiment reported in *Science* magazine last year. Natalie was trying to confirm what Bach had reported to some church congregation in Germany 250 years ago. If she did it absolutely right, it might turn out to be true. To be the truth.

That was maybe the most important thing that happened to me that day – understanding that.

After about forty minutes of practising, she started on a sticky fast part and fought with it for a while and got mad at it and went YAARKHH! on the strings and quit. She sat down on the rug too, and we talked. I told her what I had been thinking about music and thinking, and she liked it; but she asked didn't a scientist have to keep feeling out of his thinking, whereas in music they were the same thing. That didn't seem exactly right to me but we couldn't figure out just what did happen in science. I told her about working with Miss Capswell and how neat it had been, because this was the first person I had ever met who just took it for granted you were interested in ideas. Working with her in the lab had been just about the first time in my life I didn't feel like an outsider, or self-conscious, or fake; and it was really because of that that I'd realized that no matter how I tried I was never going to be an extravert, or popular, or one of the group, so I might as well quit trying. But Miss Capswell got transferred to another school over the summer and when I came back in the autumn, school was even worse than it had been before, in a way, because I wasn't even tormenting myself with trying to be part of it any more, so there wasn't anything left at all. I didn't tell Natalie all that, that evening, of course. But we did talk a bit about school, about conformity and why it is hard to be different. She said it seemed like the only choices offered were to want to be what other people were, or to be what other people wanted you to be. Either to conform, or to obey. And that got me on to the car, and college, and my parents. She listened, and she understood perfectly about the car, but not so well about college. She said, 'Well, OK, but you wouldn't actually give up going to the place where you belong, and go to a school you don't want? I mean, why?'

'Because they expect me to.'

'But they expected wrong, didn't they?'

'I don't know. There's money, too.'

'There's loans and scholarships.'

'There's a lot of competition.'

'You're telling me!' she said, fairly sarcastically. 'So you have to compete. All you can do is try, isn't it?'

She was hard to answer. But not the way my parents were. They were hard to answer because you could never get to the real point with them, and she was hard to answer because she'd got there first. But at least she didn't leave me fighting a piece of phantom pot roast. Her mother brought us up some other kind of weird tea, and we talked some more, just sort of nothing, friendly talk, and at ten-thirty I left, figuring she might want to practise some more, because she'd said she tried to practise three hours a day. I drove around a few blocks and got home and went to bed. I was really tired. Like I'd walked a hundred miles. But the fog was gone. I went to bed and straight to sleep.

Hetero, Homo, Bi or Nothing
ROBERT WESTALL

A witty, perceptive and very honest discussion of the whole sex scene and the difference between adolescent sex then and now. Many things are better now. There was a lot of repression and guilt and ignorance a generation or two ago. Many things may be worse.

The writer discusses permissiveness, opportunity, the label of 'homo' slapped on anyone without a girl, the 'moral cowardice' of teachers who ignore what goes on in the showers, the 'unending rain of sexual knowledge and stimulation'.

'The adult world,' he says, 'has created a wilderness of opportunity in which, perhaps, boys who merely want to talk, girls who merely want an affectionate social relationship ... are *expected* by society to perform in a kind of competitive sexual Olympics ... recipe for heartbreak and loneliness.'

But there was also heartbreak and loneliness, back in those other days when fear kept you from having sex, and guilt kept you from enjoying it. Perhaps the truth is that sex can never be foolproof. Each generation copes in its own way. And each generation, however liberal, is secretly going to believe that the old ways were best.

MONICA DICKENS

*

Tony was sent along to see me because his Sixth Form work was going to bits.

I tried all the usual careers-master patter. Trouble at home? Too-demanding girlfriend? Pregnant girlfriend?

No, no, no. Just apparently a grey overall haze of vague

misery that was crumbling up not only his work but his life.

I opened my door to give him back his freedom, with that sigh of pure despair that only careers-masters know. On the very threshold he turned back.

'I think I'm homosexual.'

I closed the door again, and asked gingerly whether it was anyone in particular? Not at all, he said. It was just that he didn't want to have anything to do with girls. Brown, in his form, had it away with a different girl every weekend, and said anybody who didn't was a pouff. Brown had a lot of lads worried . . .

Inwardly, I consigned Brown to the depths of Hell. Outwardly, I trotted out the usual patter about different rates of maturing, small boys and large boys, smooth boys and hairy boys, hormones, glands, yew trees and fir trees . . . It didn't make much impression.

I put the knife in on Brown, up to the hilt. I observed tartly that in my experience, the more successful men were sexually, the *less* they were inclined to talk about it. Women had a damning phrase for the Browns of this world. All say and no do.

· Better, I told Tony to ask his Dad how old *he* was before he first took a girl out. That seemed to help a bit. At least Tony opened up far enough to say there were boys in his form worse off than himself.

Boys whom the form had diagnosed as pouffs at the age of eleven, and tormented non-stop ever since; as a reliable source of amusement during periods of boredom. I was staggered. I didn't think even psychiatrists could pick out homosexuals in the pre-adolescent stage . . .

Maybe we have the gutter-press to thank instead. There have long been learned tomes which allege that one male in seven is homosexual. This is just the kind of juicy tit-bit which the gutter press have recently pounced on for their 'sensational-revelation' features. Pre-adolescents *read* the gutter-press. Some years ago I was startled to hear my eight-year-old son announce,

'All our gang are homos, and we don't have nothing to do with those lessies.' It was good for a laugh at the time.

Trouble is, anything that children lay their hands on, whether tool, weapon or fact, they are sooner or later bound to *use*. So in this case, perhaps, the toddlers looked round their mixed primary-school class of thirty and asked, 'Who are the pouffs?'

And, of course, in any class there were always a couple of gentle non-aggressive boys who will not stick up for themselves. In my day we called them 'cissies' or 'mummy's boys'. They didn't like rough games, or join in competitions to see who could pee highest over the toilet wall. They got bullied, together with fat boys, or boys with big ears. But they only got their *share* of the never-ending torment. And they might finally get aggressive; as fat boys might one day get thin. There was hope. And it was their courage that was criticized, not their sexuality scarred with doubt forever.

Tony cheered up after that. I didn't. The mass of anxiety he'd revealed to me seemed poorly described by the phrases 'liberation' and 'permissive society'. Maybe the term 'over-exposed society' might be a better one.

You see, back in the 1940s, I was as sexually backward as Tony. Without the least *trace* of anxiety.

I didn't take a girl out till I was nineteen. Doreen was one of our Sixth Form geography set. For two years I admired her demure but considerable charms; but I'd never *spoken* to her. On the day we both left school, I asked for her phone-number. Got it with a smile, but still without a word. Knew I wouldn't get rebuffed because a month previously she'd told her girlfriend she thought I was a nice boy and it had got back to me on the class grapevine. So neither of us took any risk of losing face.

I knew exactly what to do with Doreen; back row at the pictures; an immemorial tradition. We sat side by side on a double seat, like a pair of stuffed dummies. My leg touched hers by accident and we both nearly had a fit. The film was 'For Whom the Bell Tolls'. Walked her home afterwards, declaring my undying passion for Ingrid Bergman. Doreen didn't mind; she felt the same way about Gary Cooper; and the Senior Physics Master. In return, I revealed all about Hilda the History Mistress.

After that, we got stuck in a rut. Till one day Doreen told her girlfriend that if I didn't put my arm around her in the back row of the pictures soon, she'd go *insane*. Girlfriend told her boyfriend. Boyfriend told me. Next time in the pictures, I put my arm round Doreen. She put her head on my shoulder, which was what girls did then. Dead cosy, for about ten minutes. Then it got uncomfortable, but neither of us dared stir for fear of hurting the other's feelings. Next day, I had a very sore shoulder and she had a very stiff neck.

But after that, we relaxed. We'd done all that tradition expected of us. We took long walks along the seafront in the dark; me talking, her listening. I got asked for tea frequently; got taken on family car-trips. I became the family pet, slightly superior in status to the dog. (They were very fond of their dog.) My main memory is of never stopping talking, especially to her mother, who would listen to me for hours. When we broke up, I missed Doreen's mother far more than I missed Doreen. You see, nobody had ever listened to me before; my own family were sick of what they called my 'funny ideas'.

The only parts of Doreen's charms I had explored were her face, hands and the small of her back. Yet I was *not* a mass of sexual frustration; the only agony was not being asked to tea on Boxing Day, a great Tyneside festival. Yet I remember the whole thing with nothing but fondness; so they must have given me what I needed.

In our co-ed grammar school of 1949, I was not abnormal.
We'd lived *alongside* the girls for seven years. Boys occupied
the seats by the window; girls the other half. The boys who
sat next to the girls, and vice-versa, were the unlucky late-
comers. All but Billy Turner, who *always* sat next to the
girls. We despised Billy as a *dirty* boy. He not only whispered
to the girls all the time; he told dirty jokes. Not *doubles-
entendres*, or sexy puns, at which we all worked hard, but
jokes in which men actually *did* things to women. But then
he was not normal. He was a bully. Bad at schoolwork and
didn't care. Never played games for the school and didn't
care. Frequently said out loud that he was the son of a
labourer and proud of it. When, at sixteen, he went to a
holiday-camp and got a factory-girl pregnant, and had to
leave school to marry her, we primly pursed our lips and said
(echoing our grandmothers) that it was a Judgement. It
confirmed our beliefs that the real purpose of life was being
top in Latin, or playing for the County XV.

I suppose Brown and Billy Turner were brothers under the
skin. The precocious, quickly maturing few. In the 1940s,
society was against them, even persecuted them. Now,
society allows them to persecute others. It doesn't seem much
of an improvement.

But don't get the idea that we were sexually *oppressed* by
adults. Parents and teachers never mentioned sex at all; so we
thought it mustn't be all that important. Even the biology
master never mentioned sex (though Billy Turner said he had
a female rat in his stock-cupboard, drowned in alcohol, and
cut open to reveal sex-organs tinted blue). Society expected us
to compete in schoolwork and games. This left scars enough –
I have a permanently crippled left knee, and an insatiable
hunger for intellectual TV quizzes. Show me 'University
Challenge' and I drool at the mouth like a Pavlovian dog. But
at least society left me sexually unscarred by undue expectation.

What do I mean, undue sexual expectation? Well, some years ago, as a teacher, I attended a mixed course for teachers and Sixth-Formers. One evening, we teachers were sitting in the bar when one of us came in and said, 'The Sixth are having an orgy in the showers.' Nobody went to investigate (though there were Heads among us). We *wanted* to believe that all the Sixth were happy ravers. We huddled closer in a defensive circle over our beer, and didn't want to look. It was only later, in bed, that I recalled that the showers were narrow cells of wet concrete. Rather a *poor* place for an orgy ... But suppose there had been an orgy, and one of the girls hadn't really wanted to, but the rest had cried 'no guts' or 'frigid' or 'lessy'? The young are great competers and compliers ...

Was what we teachers did permissive or downright moral cowardice? Isn't adult society putting terrible pressures on adolescents in three ways? We expect them to mature earlier, to be ravers. We give them unlimited access to sexual possibilities, and we subject them to an unending rain of sexual knowledge and stimulation.

On the matter of access, for instance, adolescents are terribly vulnerable. What you give a young person, he will sooner or later be impelled to use. Leave fags lying about loose and you will make him a smoker. Leave loose change lying about and you will make him a petty thief. Leave opportunity for sex lying about ...

In my time, many a strict father told his daughter that she had to be home by ten or he'd half kill her. This did not stop some girls having sex if they *wanted* it badly enough; some did get pregnant. But if a girl *didn't* want to, a strict dad was a marvellous alibi. Whereas I know of a boy who got his girl pregnant after her parents had left them alone together in the house five nights a week till nearly midnight for nearly a year. Who planned *that* pregnancy? And I hear from at least one London comprehensive that a very strict watch has to be kept on the school gates at lunchtime, or fourteen-year-olds will slip away to make love in their parents' bedrooms. Latchkeys were always potent sexual symbols.

In other words, the adult world has created a wilderness of opportunity in which, perhaps, boys who merely want to talk, girls who merely want an affectionate social relationship with a bit of snog, are *expected* by society to perform in a kind of competitive sexual Olympics. I cannot think of a better recipe for heartbreak and loneliness . . .

But perhaps the barrage of sexual knowledge is worse. Back in the forties, we lads did a lot of touching. We paraded round in pairs, arms round each others necks, for hours. Who would dare do that today? There was a lot of wrestling in the bath after rugby. The scrum-half used to dance the can-can clad only in school-tie, spectacles and boots. Friendships were deep and painful; hearts got broken there all right. I vied for years with a wing-threequarter for the 'best-friendship' of the fullback, and I still hate that wing-three to this day, though we are all now much-married men.

But nobody pointed the two fingers of scorn. A pouff was something you sat on, by the fire of a winter's night. I came across the word 'homosexual' in a book my father kept hidden in the sideboard, under the biscuit-tin and Christmas sherry. Doing Latin, I soon worked its meaning out. 'Homo' meant man, and sexual meant sexual. So a homosexual was someone who made love to a man, in other words a woman. Since the book was hidden from me, and therefore risqué, homosexuals must be female prostitutes . . . I never worried about the word again until I joined the Samaritans at the age of thirty-five. The media was no more interested in homosexuals than in Flat-Earthers or Seventh-Day Adventists.

Of course, we all knew men who went on living with their mothers or married sisters until far into middle-age. They were accepted gently as being 'old bachelors' or 'tongue-tied with women'. Nobody cast aspersions. In fact, much-married men were heard at times to envy their common-sense out loud ... Unmarried female schoolteachers were expected to live in pairs 'for company'. Even unmarried men teachers. Sherlock Holmes dwelt peaceably with Doctor Watson ... how soon before some avant-garde playwright portrays *them* as a pair of pouffs?

In this spate of homosexual frankness, I don't know how male friendship survives at all.

It seems to survive, in a mangled form. My son of seventeen does not go out with girls. He goes out with a lot of boys, on motorbikes. His friends arrive at all hours, clad in the identical faded jeans, black leather jackets and yellow crash-helmets. I sometimes open the front door to them, shouting 'Have you forgotten your bloody front-door key *again*?' They lie about our lounge with their massive boots on the furniture, eating any food made available, talking, talking, talking about sprockets and baffles, cogging-down and doing a ton. Sometimes they go to rallies in Morecambe, where they drink illegally and walk about in large groups, bristling with machismo and having minor brushes with a fairly tolerant police-force. It never gets beyond rocking panda-cars on their suspension and whistling the Z-cars theme sarcastically. They risk their lives a lot on the road – some have broken collar-bones and worse. They are brave and hard and spend a great deal of energy proving it. If anyone called them pouffs, they'd probably beat him to a pulp. Yet they have no time for girls outside nuddy-books.

What worries me a bit is that they never display the slightest sign of affection for each other. To hear my son talking down the phone to a friend, you would think he was talking to his worst enemy. If Chris stays up half the night helping a friend mend his bike, he insists it is because of interest in the job – not friendship. You might think, to hear them, that they were one of the milder groups of the Waffen SS, or Cromwell's brutal and licentious soldiery. Monumental and apocalyptic rudeness is the common mode of address. Apart and together, they run down each other's characters endlessly and mercilessly. Yet behind their eyes are the same happy, affectionate children that we saw four years ago. Only they never, never show it. They *still* feel the need for physical contact with each other – but it comes out as a kind of savage wrestling – an excruciating form of tickling. Horrible – I know because I occasionally suffer it. And yet I know that behind it lies affection that *dare* not show itself. The only reason you can tell they are friends is that they persist in keeping company. Yet they are the nicer kind of grammar-school boys. Over-awareness, starting at the age of eight, of homosexuality seems to have raised the famous English taboo on tenderness to lunatic heights. Anything to prove you're not a pouff ...

Their time is running out. Soon, I suppose, some enterprising young woman will coax my son into taking her for a ride, professing a *passionate* interest in bikes. In reality, she will be taking him for a ride, because her main purpose will be to get him to exchange the bike for a car. All I can say is that I won't envy her job in civilizing him. Maybe she won't mind living in a house that resembles a mechanical knacker's-yard. What worries me more is that he will be starting his education in tenderness, affection, talking about his real feelings, sensitivity, *terribly* late. I started to learn to love girls by loving boys first, and I don't mean homosexuality.

But what about the young men who go on being *non-sexual?* Like a university-lecturer friend of mine who was still *nothing* at age thirty. Then he began taking a tremendous interest in homosexuals and their problems. He literally threw himself into homosexual society. A month later, he threw himself out again; something had happened, that he never spoke about, that had convinced him he wasn't homosexual. Within a month, he was having a totally satisfying affair with a Chinese nurse. The point was that she was equally shocking, equally a bloody nose for his domineering mother, who had spent all those years insisting that he settle down and raise a family with some nice white Anglo-Saxon. He's all right now; but I hate to think what he had to go through, because our media-inflamed society insisted that he had to be *something* – hetero, homo, bi-sexual ... you've got to belong to a team. Is that permissiveness? Is that freedom?

There remains the loneliness of the boy who finally has to admit he is homosexual. Our society is growing more tolerant, but in funny treacherous ways. Once, I gave a preparation-talk to a bunch of Samaritan trainees on helping homosexuals. Very enlightened, very compassionate ... or so I thought. One trainee, a retired bank-manager, walked out in a rage, accusing me of running a homosexual brothel. He didn't worry me – we couldn't have used him anyway. The trainee who shook me was the one who stayed after the rest had gone, and said, 'I was very interested in your talk – you see, I *am* homosexual.' I asked him what he'd thought of my talk. He said,

'Society used to regard us as monsters to be punished. Now you regard us as cripples to be pitied.'

He had a point. He made me see why homosexuals have become so militant. Why some say that homosexual sex is *better* than hetero. But such militancy doesn't help their relationships with heteros.

What I do know is that it is very bad to define people by their sexuality alone. I don't mind people saying 'Westall hates buying new clothes' or even 'Westall picks fluff out of his navel for a hobby'. But if they started cocking an eyebrow and saying 'He's a *heterosexual* of course' I would start getting narked. My sexuality is only a small part of me; it *doesn't* explain my whole being.

That is why I suspect that temptation which Samaritans have had in the past to help lonely homosexuals by directing them to where they can find other homosexuals. If, as a lonely hetero, someone sent me to a bunch of heteros who drank like fish, talked only about Manchester United and referred to women as 'slags' ... I wouldn't thank them. I'd rather spend my time with an intelligent homosexual who liked listening to Vivaldi, discussing poetry and playing backgammon. Homosexuals are *persons* first. If they insist in banding together in militant groups, will they not create homosexual ghettos? Better, if possible, to mix with everybody.

But before you start, comes the burning question 'To reveal, or not to reveal?' Our present media-inflamed society encourages people to reveal *all*. Anything else is to be a coward, a hypocrite. Yet heteros, like Brown and Billy Turner, who flaunt their sexuality in everyone's face, are never popular. Sexual flaunting is *not* a basis for friendship. On the other hand, a lot of heteros, particularly those partial to adultery, actually seem to enjoy secrecy, saying it gives an edge to the sexual experience. I know there is an air of homosexual *crusading* around at the moment; but the point about crusades, or great causes, is that they tend to make martyrs, or ruin people's personal lives. Look what happened to the Suffragettes, or the family of Karl Marx ... Do you *really* want to give your life for the cause?

And into the bargain, inflict on your father, mother, granny and Uncle Tom Cobley and all, the burden of adjusting to your homosexuality when they are simply too set in their ways to do so.

On the other hand, if you do want to stay a part of multi-sexual society, where do you look for your friends? Oddly enough – perhaps among hetero women. Hetero women tend at times to get rather fed up with the coarse grabbiness of many heterosexual men – beer, betting, football, making money. They appreciate someone who cares about personal relationships, fine things, art, poetry.

Friendship with heterosexual men is rather harder.

They're usually terrified you might fancy them. This is not, as some homosexuals would have you think, because heteros fear they contain pits of homosexuality which your sexual advances would reveal. It is merely the good old English fear of inappropriateness which leads to embarrassment. Like having a woman you can't stand make a heavy pass at you . . . The best friendship I had with a homosexual man started with him saying.

'I don't fancy *you*, you know. I've got *some* taste . . .' We laughed like drains, and got on like a house on fire after that.

We live in a society containing two kinds of tolerance. There is the new acceptance, still partial, still forming. But there is also the old tolerance, dying but still there, that really wants to turn a blind eye if you don't force the fact of your homosexuality down its throat. Between them, you should make out. I am convinced that in twenty years' time no one will care whether you're homosexual or not. Till then, perhaps, it's best a case of softly softly. Your sexuality, hetero or homo, is, in the end, no one's concern but your own.

Transit Passengers

JANE GARDAM

Above a Cretan seashore, very young hippies from all over Europe and America live in caves in the ledges of the mountain 'like swallows under a barn roof'. The villagers wonder that they exist without work, and are openly lovers, passive in each other's arms on the beach or in the swallow's nests above the crashing sea. Tourists come in a bus to stare at them.

Now three of them are at the airport, going home. The bearded mole to a Jewish grandmother in New York, tall Mark, getting on the plane with bare feet and sand-matted hair to a rich father in Hong Kong, the slow peaceful girl back to Mummy in Tunbridge Wells, and the new kittens and coffee shops and the scholarly commitment of Cambridge.

This story seems to be saying, 'You must go home', but is it really saying, like Thomas Wolfe, 'You can't go home again'? Or is it saying, 'You can go home, but not as the same person'? This is one of those stories your mind continues after the words have stopped.

MONICA DICKENS

*

'So, if it goes it goes.'

'Yes.'

The rare bus was coming, ramshackle, in a cloud of dust, bright blue against the blocks of rock and blocks of small white houses. A man on a tall mule drew in to the side of the preposterous road. He was regal, with a hero's moustache, and did not turn to see whether his wife who walked behind, a bent witch over a long stick, or the white silk goat who walked behind her would be able to draw in, too. The bus passed in a brown cloud and stopped by the sea shore car-park where the three students waited.

'It's here,' called the tall fair boy.

The dark girl got into the bus.

'Come on,' called the tall boy to the other one – a small American, bearded, bespectacled, reading a book, detached as a mole. In the bus all three had to sit separately in odd seats among the peasants, some with loaves and some with hens, and the tourists in their silver earrings bought in Aghios Nicolaus with their sun-tans and guide books who had come out here to see the hippies. The girl, big, with a wide shield of a face and a long dress made out of red and grey striped rough cotton, sat staring in front of her. Her eyes were dark and wide – very bright. She sat with knees apart under her long dress, easy, her arm touching the arm of the old man next to her but not noticing. The tall boy thought, she breathes out peace. Her luggage which neither of the boys had helped her with was on her knees – a canvas sack. From each side of her head above her ears scraps of hair coiled and twisted. They must have tickled her cheeks but she held the sack and did not tuck them away. Her legs were bare. She wore open-toed sandals dried and hard as old seaweed. The tall boy had bare feet. The mole wore jeans, striped ankle socks and some leather shoes his grandmother had sent him from New York. Mark, the tall one, and the girl, Cassy, stared ahead, bumping and thumping and rocketing about the bus. The mole read.

They could not sit together in the plane either. It was a student charter flight and packed. Some were drunk and some were drunk with sun. Some were noisy and some complained of the service. At Athens they poured out and streamed with plastic parcels and bottles and string bags over the tarmac to the main building.

'Your plane's in half an hour,' said Mark to Cassy.

Cassy shifted her pack from hand to hand. They stood together in the place kept for transit passengers. 'I can never

remember what it means,' said Cassy looking out at the
Greek mountains, scalloped and pink, so different from the
crags of Crete. ' "Transit passengers". We all are.'

'Not if we've arrived.'

'Who's arrived?'

'Well – if you're stopping. Not going on.'

'It's not possible though is it?' She speaks so slowly he
thought, she sometimes sounds almost stupid. For three
months he had lived with her inside a Cretan mountain: on a
shelf, in a fault in the shale, like swallows under a barn roof,
except that the faults, the nests, were one beneath another
down the rock, envelopes, like mille-feuilles. In each lifted
envelope of rock the hippies lived, making a cave for themselves with some sort of a bed. Some hung a curtain or made a
screen of branches, bought a gaz to cook with and a pan.
They had a bad name. It said in the guide books that they
begged in the villages and that the Cretans who had been
used to giving hospitality since the days of Minos were now
beginning to wonder why. The villagers watched the hippies
– even now not knowing what hippies were – how they slept
in the eaves of the mountain looking down at the clean,
gritty beach where the clean green waves reared and crashed
and sucked, publicly sleeping up there at odd hours, coming
down late in the night to play music on guitars and lie about
the sand drinking Pepsis out of tins. They were quiet enough
people. The Cretan villagers were quiet, too, but bewildered
by the openness of the young lovers. For they all were lovers.
They all loved each other. They seemed half asleep and
played poor music and draggled in long clothes, did without
shoes and never went near the church and spent their time
washing, washing, washing their bodies and their clothing
and sucking at the sweet cigarettes. They never fought or
were jealous or worked. Money now and then came out of the
plastic folders – you took them to Heraklion and signed your
name and came back on the bus with a wad of drachs. But

they loved one another, the Cretans wonderingly acknowledged, watching the lanky English and Americans and big-boned Scandinavians sitting together in clusters or lying in each other's arms in the swallows' nests above the crashing sea. More like sleeping than loving, the Cretans thought. More like dying than sleeping.

'So, if it goes it goes?' he said. 'You're sure?'

She was going back to London now – non-stop Heathrow 21 hours 30. Tunbridge Wells by midnight. The mole would be with her till Heathrow where he would consider. It would be New York then or New York later. Because of his grandmother (Monty – the mole – was a New York Jew who never spoke: a phenomenon). He had a First at Cambridge and a scholarship to take up either at Yale or Johns Hopkins. He was looking after Cassy for Mark till Heathrow.

'Look after Cassy,' said Mark, tall as a giraffe among the running Greeks, bright as Achilles, wretched as Achilles. 'Hey Monty, look after Cassy.' Monty put away the book on revolutions. He came just about to Cassy's shoulder. She was a tall girl and moved slowly. Her eyes at present were bright and not quiet. 'Cassy looks after me,' he said, 'She – '

'Cassy,' Mark said, 'you're sure I'm to go?'

They had slept together and lazed together from July to the end of September and he was going East for a year to his father who was a Hong Kong solicitor, she West, home to Kent, then to Cambridge. It was the time they call the best time of your life between school and university. They were both nineteen. The mole, already through with Cambridge and, so he said, with most things, was twenty-three. He sat apart with his back to them and got the history book out again. Above their head a Greek voice began to cry out in frenzy over a loud-speaker. Round them people started running.

'It's your plane,' he said, 'I think.'

'Yes,' she said, 'I want the *Guardian*.'

'It may not be yours.'

'Yes it is. It's 603. I've learned some Greek. Thanks Mont.'

'Some Cretan.'

'Not much. I've not learned much. Not much more than before.'

'Look,' he said, 'I can still come back. Now. I don't have to go to my bloody father. I don't want filthy Hong Kong. It's just there's nowhere – '

'You've not seen him for two years.'

'His fault. He's got the money. He's a bloody rich lawyer.'

'No.'

'He's thick.'

'You don't know him.'

'He plays golf all the time.'

'Mark – you might get to China. That's why – '

'Yes,' he said, with such a knell of woe she laughed, and her large face grew alive and joyous. 'Oh Mark! China!'

'I don't want China. I want you. I can't do without you, Cassy, now.'

They stood together as the crowds went by and the Greek voice in the metal box yelled above them. 'It's been three months, Cassy.'

'Nothing.'

'I'll come back. In the spring I expect. I'll write every few days.'

'No.'

'I have to. I'll die. I'll have no one to talk to. This thing – us – I think.'

'What?' She was almost alight with laughter beneath the skin, her eyes almost tearful, watching such a comedy.

'I think it's going to last with us,' he said, 'a *long* time.'

'What – through Hong Kong and Cambridge?'

'Yes. It won't stop. For me it won't stop.'

The mole pocketed the revolutions and took a can of Coke

from his pocket. 'When you gotta go you gotta go,' he remarked, taking a swig. The announcer was becoming almost
hysterical with anxiety. From the midst of the frantic chatter
of starling Greek even names could now be distinguished.
'Miss Casseee Veeessee, Miss Cassseee Veeeeseeee, Mr Monty
Fogelburg, Mr Monteee Fogel – '

'If it goes,' she said, coming across to Mark slowly in her
long dress and putting down her sack which Monty gathered
up. 'If it goes – '

'C'mon Cassy,' Monty said, chucking the can in a bin. He
had spoken thrice. It was an emergency. 'C'mon Cass.'

'If it goes,' she said calmly putting both arms round Mark's
neck high above her and laying her head against the rough
queer Arab robe she had made for him out of some stuff from
Marshall and Snelgrove – 'If it goes, then of course it goes.'

He clutched her and said, 'It – I can't – it won't stop. This
is for a long time.'

But she released herself and they were gone through the
barrier towards their plane. Monty turned as they reached
the farther check-in where they began to be searched in the
familiar way for drugs and bombs – passport pictures carefully checked against faces, luggage scattered, picked over by
people who should never never see it – should never see
Cassy's most secret possessions which were so few and spare
and good because she believed only in beauty and transience
and the giving away of as much as possible and in no ties.
Mark knew everything in Cassy's sack – some cotton shirts, a
long cotton skirt, pants, a jersey for a cold day, a comb, soap,
shampoo, *The Prophet* by Kahlil Gibran which Monty
laughed at, and a picture of her niece. At first there had been
a double photograph of a heavy, jowled man and a woman
beginning to go at the neck with a troubled face and pearl
earrings, but these had gone. There were a dozen lemons, a
bottle of honey and a postcard he had given her of the
Minoan girl dug up at Knossos, the girl with the ringlets and

the reckless mouth. He had written on the back, 'This is Cassy'.

He waited for them to be given back their belongings at the further gate – his plane for Beirut, Bangkok, Hong Kong was not for ages. He waited for them to be signed off and hustled towards England and to turn and wave. He could still just see them at the end of the transit section but the Greek police were taking their time with Monty. Beards mean pot. Thin American students with beards who do not speak and carry books on revolutions could mean heroin. Neither Cassy nor Mark nor Monty used anything, not even alcohol, not even meat, but always waited patiently through these formalities, indeed would have been insulted had they been considered unworthy of them. Monty was putting all the things back in his bag slowly and neatly. Cassy's beautiful broad back and long trail of hair could be seen beside him. Now they were through. She would turn.

But she did not. The two of them spoke briefly together and nodded. They each picked up their luggage and hurried off without looking back.

'She's gone,' he thought. 'She's not with me any more.'

His plane swooped up off the airport and swept like a swallow above the pink mountains. In a moment the airport was gone, only the fluted mountains lay bright in the evening light shadowed like upturned patty tins, the sea ridiculously blue, ridiculously white-fringed and postcard-like beside them.

Her plane was far away now. Above Italy now, over Rome. Or Florence. She's pointing out the Duomo, the Po valley. The Alps are coming up, have passed – the dull green plains and parquet fields of France. Tonight the standard roses on the lawn, lattice windows, the spaniel, roast chicken. 'Oh darling it's lovely to have you back. Oh such a long time. Plenty of hot water. How was Mark? And Monty? Such a character!'

Oh I want you Cassy Cassy.

Oh I want you in our cave.

She's going up the stairs now in the red dress. ('Darling – that dress! Do you never wear anything else? However long since it was washed? There are three kittens. Hurry down.') She walks heavily and looks down from the half landing – still face, watchful eyes. Oh Cassy you never say a word you do not mean. Oh Cassy you are all hard sense. 'All right Mark, it's love if you like. But if it goes, it goes.'

'But you see what I mean Cassy? It's a test. If it lasts now – I love you, naturally.'

'Naturally?'

'Don't laugh. I don't see why I shouldn't say love. I do love you Cassy. But if I come back to England now – Well, I'll be back anyway next year – '

'What I'm saying Cassy is, if it's going to be a – well, last a *long* time, well then, it'll last a *long* time. Won't it?'

'But if it's going to go,' she said, calm as a Greek sea under the moon, 'then it will go.'

There were dirty Arabs at Beirut with skeins of black wool round their heads. Air-hostesses all knife-pleats and paint and hair-lacquer pranced about, directing them with distaste. Australians drank out of bottles and shouted. The lights of Beirut twinkled in an arc around the great bay, higher and higher about the hills. Mark lay with his head on his pack and his eyes shut in the big dark lounge. The 747 was going to be late. Work out the time for Cassy. Long past midnight, nearly morning, she sleeping, her window shut against the cold after Crete; outside it all the apples of Kent hanging away and away like round gold jewels decorating the Weald. Her bed will have clean sheets, the old dress dropped on the floor in a heap. She might be in a nightdress. Cassy in clothes in bed! Under his yellow beard he smiled.

'Flight to Bangkok.' The stewardess said sharply at his shoulder, 'Quickly.'

They sat in a block. An old American of tremendous size beside him asked for whisky. 'I wanna *bottle* of whisky,' he said. 'Yeah. And I want it now. A bottle. Right. And now bring me a glass.' He poured a paper carton she brought full of whisky to the brim and swilled it down as the plane took off. He held the bottle in one hand and the carton in the other, not being allowed to use his tray in case the plane crashed and it sliced him in half. 'I start with whisky,' he said to Mark. 'I always gotta be drunk before I can go down to Singapore.' He pronounced it '*Si*ngapore'.

'It's Hong Kong,' said Mark, alarmed, 'isn't it?'

'That's right. Hong Kong.'

He began to pour a second carton and wag his head. A Chinese sitting near moved no muscle. The pupil and the iris of their eyes are one, Mark thought. 'Ya hippy then?' asked the American. 'Jesus people? Can't give you any of this then. You'll be on the other stuff.' Without one hint of movement from muscle, nerve or bone Mark felt the disgust of the Chinese for the American. His interest stirred.

'Like this gang here,' said the fat man pointing at the Chinese and now very drunk. 'Keep it in the heels of their shoes. Any rate, you can't do that.' He wheezed with laughter and pushed a foot towards Mark's bare feet. Mark shrank and catching the Chinese's eyes felt sympathy. He nodded at him and the Chinese bowed gravely back. Only when the lights of the plane went out and the American slept did he put on the British Airways blue socks and then very surreptitiously and only because it was cold.

She'll be in bed for breakfast. She'll have the dog on the bed. There'll be toast and stuff – marmalade. The telephone'll be going. 'Is Cassy back?' She won't be caring – dump the tray on the floor, turn over, sleep, sleep. Such a heavy sleeper. Says so little. She's so strong. Can get on without anyone. But I was her first.

In Bangkok though there were the great gold hats of the

workmen – huge, rising to a pricked point and the faces beneath red like Red Indians, slant-eyed and pointed too. Thin, thin arms. Christ the heat as you go over the tarmac! Even the girls behind the gift stalls have their heads in their arms – but they bob up and grin when they think you'll buy. The men outside are building something with a scaffolding of grass. But talk, talk, talk. The Thai girl at the foot of the gangway as we go back is tiny. Comes to my waist just about. She has eyes like small black lemons and round lips smiling. Talk, talk. Soft as a bird. Yet thin as a flake. She has a big gun in her belt.

Cassy will be drinking Nescafé. With that girl she knows who's going to Oxford. In the coffee shop in Tunbridge Wells. Or wait a minute, it'll be tomorrow won't it? Or will it be last night? She's that God-awful girl anyway with the brown teeth.

We are coming down low now over the China Sea. To the north is the coast of Vietnam. It is red and yellow – quite peaceful. A quiet coast. Like an orange Belgium. The sea is as still as a floor, waveless. The Miekong delta must flow into it somewhere – all that blood. All that pain. The Cambodians live in a desert now with spikes instead of trees – spikes like gibbets and holes for the twisted dead. The Cambodians were dignified people who wore top hats. Cassy and Monty used to go on about it. All those bombs and lasers and bullets. The noise of it. You'd never think, looking at that pale bit of coast –

Cassy will be –

The sky's changing. There's a great grey cumulus ahead like – God, like Europe. Like Newcastle. Or like Lille. Or like filthy Warwick. (Why didn't I stay another year at school and try for Cambridge. Christ, Warwick!)

The sun's gone. We're going down. I've been asleep. We're going down into the sea. Hey – the skyscrapers! Look at them. All of a sudden Europe. Or Manhattan. Out there just standing in the sea! Cliffs again with rows of little holes down them, neat round holes in the great tall pencils. All crowded up together. Hey it's Lego – it's not buildings. And in between there's shacks, bits of leaves over sticks. We're nearly touching them. All the washing hanging out. Hey it's wonderful!

The vast American was asleep with the bottle and the carton, one in each hand, at an angle. The air hostess who had joined them at Bangkok whisked them out of his hands, buttoned up his tray as she went by on light feet. As tiny as the Thai but more precise, prouder. The bones of her head were minute, perfect, her quickness lovely. The Chinese alongside him had seen him thinking again, and again catching Mark's eye he bowed.

There was a Rolls the size of a room waiting, with gold headlamps and the driver in white with gold buttons. Mark's father reading the *Financial Times*, dressed as if for Chancery Lane, stood beside it. 'Dear Mark,' he said. 'I'm not long out of court. Bless you. Where's the luggage?'

With every sign of pleasure the gold and white chauffeur picked up Mark's stained sack. 'All done? All finished?' his father asked. 'Searched for drugs and all that rubbish? What a world. Well done.'

In the car they swam beneath concrete bridges, swept through streets of soft green and red and gold Chinese neon signs. The streets were being swung back and forth by great waves of small dark people all hurrying, smiling, elbowing, talking. Before the hotel a fountain played, green and gold and pink by turns in front of huge glass doors and a sugar-cake Empire façade. Little boys in white with white pill-box hats hauled back the doors like clockwork dolls. Inside a huge garden grew among the tea-tables in a circle of marble (or was it jade?) and roses and lilies and ferns and orchids were banked up in it under a glass-domed roof. At the hundred tables people sipped drinks and ate French cakes. Talk, talk. Outside by the great flight of main steps a little dark-yellow cadaver of a man, with fingers like something you suck off the bone with rice, made magically, with small pointed movements, grasshoppers out of green leaves with baby grasshoppers woven in to their backs. Mark saw not far away something else – a human head resting on a low heap of brown blankets and thought my God it's food! It's food for sale. They're cannibals. But the head with long matted hair turned slowly towards him. It was a Mongolian face, sleepy, peaceful and filthy. In front of the man on the pavement magazines were spread out for sale and a rat ran over them.

'There,' said his father. 'Baggage seen to. Not much of it. Have to get you some more belongings. It gets cold here. Can you change for dinner? Doesn't matter.' He was smiling at Mark – not a word about the Arab robe, the beard and hair sticky with Cretan sand nor – good God! – the aeroplane socks which he'd forgotten to take off. His father was smiling with delight at him. 'By God it's nice to see you old love,' he said. 'You're three feet taller.'

'We'll go to the Kowloon when you've washed. I live in the hotel at present – since your mother left – but we won't always eat here. Get you used to some chop-sticks tonight. Tomorrow I'll take you up to have a look across at China.'

A small Chinese of such immaculate appearance that Mark thought he must be one of his father's senior partners approached, and with great reverence and pleasure held out a tray with a telegram on it.

'What's this?' said his father. 'For me? No, for you. For my son.'

'This is not one son but two son,' said the telegraph boy shaking with respectful laughter and keeping his eyes politely off Mark's feet. 'One son on other son's shoulder.'

'I think I've got jet-lag,' said Mark,' 'I feel a bit off.' He pulled the telegram slowly out of its thick yellow envelope.

'Crete to Athens took ages. Then at Beirut, ages. Then nine hours to Bangkok, then Bangkok – '

The telegram said, 'I love you I love you Oh I love you It is for ever Cassy.'

'You'll feel odd for a day or two,' his father said. 'The difference in time. I hope it's nothing?'

'Nothing?'

'Your telegram.'

They were being taken up in a blue and gold lift to a room with twelve-foot pure-silk curtains and a bathroom of black marble.

'No, nothing,' said Mark, 'Just a girl.'

'Plenty of those,' said his father.

Mark groped for Cassy. He trod the deep carpet, looked in the bathroom. A white telephone stood on the black bath. There were five fat white towels over gold rails, an acre of mirror. Cassy was not there.

'It's fantastic,' he said, opening a cupboard full of drink, another which was a television set, another which was a stereo, another which was a desk. (Cassy was not there.) 'It's wonderful!' He looked across a bay of lights that stretched to heaven.

'I could stay here,' he said, 'a *long* time.'

They smiled at one another, man to man.

Take-Off Point
ROY BROWN

Keith's predicament is horrible. He asks for help, but what help could ever be enough to put his life right again? At first reading, the gentle ending may seem like an evasion. Nothing has been solved, no practical help given, the small success can't change anything. Second thoughts show the kind of contact that has been achieved. Ted has not demanded courage of Keith, he has expected it. The small success of facing the people is nothing by itself, but it could be a door opening on the future.

MONICA DICKENS

*

He tried three telephone boxes before going through with it. They were widely separated in the rain-hazed streets. He approached each not with the brisk haste of someone bent upon making a simple call but with many doublings back and hunched journeys round unnecessary corners.

On the way he had paused under no lamp post, nor lingered in lighted shop doorways. Nowadays he embraced the darkness, but by his own choice, like a blind man or a creature inhabiting the ocean's depths. Even the soft, public glow of the kiosks dismayed him: he'd hesitated before them as if each might be wired to a detonator.

The first line was engaged and he'd waited no longer than ten seconds. At the next phone the answering signal had bleeped like a fuse in his brain. When a woman's voice had answered he'd crouched there paralytically breathing into the mouthpiece before slamming the handset on its rest.

At the third kiosk the voice responded at once. 'Samaritans, here. Can I help you?'

Still he couldn't bring himself to speak. He felt his own hot breath on his slit of mouth and the question was repeated without agitation or haste or demand.

He said, at last, 'I don't know. Feel a bit stupid bothering you.'

'No bother. That's what I'm here for. Waiting for calls.'

A young voice, neither indifferent nor intrusive.

'I saw your number on a poster. I had to talk to somebody. Feel a bit scared, see? Of myself, this thing that keeps clanking around in my mind. It's not that I want to do it . . . it just keeps clanking round in my mind.'

'Where are you?' The slightest hint of urgency, now.

'Does it matter?'

'Just thought, if you was near enough, you might fancy coming along to the Centre. Nobody much about. There's a room where we could chew things over.'

'I can't.'

'Let's talk on the phone then.'

'I can't. I need help. Can you come to me?'

'I might. I'll have to check. Is it still raining?'

'Drizzling a bit. If you don't want to get wet . . .'

'Hang on a minute. Yes, look it's OK. I can come.'

'Where shall we meet?'

'Dunno – Fancy a jar? Could meet in a pub.'

He felt suddenly over-exposed in the phone box, a shape caught in a searchlight. A blurred figure hovered grey and impatient, breathing on the glass. 'I'll hang around. Corner of Remington Street, opposite Woolworths. How will I know you?'

'Just look for a cloud of exhaust smoke, mate. I've got the sort of motor bike they use to prop up a museum door. By the way, the name's Ted.'

'Keith,' he said. He forced himself to open the kiosk door, turning away from a woman peering at him through misted spectacles.

He slouched into the wet street, already on the run again, regretting his impulse. Sod Ted, or whatever his name was. He'd probably think the call had been a hoax. Hard lines, *mate*.

But the renewed darkness soothed him. After all, he'd made some sort of decision at last, taken one step back from the gallows he had built in his mind. No point in dodging this bloke now.

He felt no particular curiosity about 'Ted'. Some trendy young curate? Red-brick cockney, 'mate' and all. Pink and earnest face shining with clean living above a carefully scruffy leather jacket; or his face full of hair to show that he was One of Us. He'd probably raise his tankard like a communion cup and talk about Bonhoeffer.

To hell with the pub, though. His digs would be better.

The motor bike emerged out of the bits of traffic. Rider wearing a white helmet – what else? Late-twentieth-century substitute for a parson's collar!

The rider spluttered past with a brief wave, apparently having no trouble picking out Keith, whatever the population of London. He pulled up, leapfrogging across the pavement, and chained his bike to the railings. 'Keith?'

'Hi.'

'I wouldn't let a cat out on a night like this.' Small, slight figure with shoulder-length straw-coloured hair sprouting under his helmet. No handshake, hardly a glance. *Had he noticed yet?*

'Let's get out of the weather.'

'I was thinking . . .' began Keith, but the bloke was striding across the street, apparently knowing where he was heading. One pub, garish and brilliant-fronted, piped rock music throbbing across the street. Ted ignored this one, found a second. Green Dragon.

The place had an air of amiable decadence. Not too crowded, yet. The lights over the bar glistened on rows of bottles but the interior receded into a hinterland of shadowy glass-topped tables and shabby green chairs. Ted led Keith to the dimmest corner and took off his helmet. 'What's yours, mate?'

'Half a bitter, thanks.'

Ted came back with two beers and sat down opposite Keith as if to throw an extra shadow across the table.

He'd got it by now! Nothing so crude as a raise of eyebrows, nothing you could call pity on his face. Thank Christ for that, at least! Ted, doing his bit for society, would no doubt settle those bright, clear eyes of his with just such detachment upon an Antiguan reptile.

'Well, cheers.'

'Cheers.'

Silence between them; through from the public bar a juke box was playing, not too loud.

Eventually Keith said, 'I thought they'd send somebody different.'

'Different?'

'Older, for a start.'

Ted said, 'I was the one who got the call. So I came.'

'Well, thanks for taking the trouble. Now we're here, where do we start?'

'Start what?'

'Talking. I thought you blokes were supposed to be hot on the old yak-yak?'

'What do you want to know?'

'Isn't it what you want that matters?'

Keith couldn't get used to the gaze. It was a long time since anybody had looked at him like this. As if . . . 'You wouldn't happen to know a good plastic surgeon? Cheapish?'

'Not offhand. I could find out.'

'Stupid to ask. Just trying to get the conversation going. Take-off point, like.'

'Sure. Take off as soon as you fancy.'

'It was last summer. I had a motor bike, too. Suzuki. Went on a tour of Spain, solo. You know Spain?'

'Lake District's my limit.'

'I'd been there for a couple of weeks, reckoned on making it a month altogether. I thought I was getting to know my way around. One day, I was on this coast road with the Med. on my left. Not much traffic. I kept out of the tourist spots as much as I could. Always was a bit of a loner. I found this village down on the coast. Forget the name of it. Steep winding road out into the mountains. One morning, I chugged the Suzuki all the way to the top. No problem. It was coming back it happened. All day I'd felt pretty good – free, you know? You don't get the same feeling in the Lake District. I'd left it a bit late coming back down. Had a lot of gear with me because there was nowhere else to leave it. Tent, stove, usual sort of thing. I should have kept my speed down with that load on my pillion but something got into me. Road winding down through the trees, nothing in sight except dicky birds. I must have been even more of a bloody fool than usual . . . touched eighty on the bend. Then, suddenly, there was this Spanish coach grinding up towards me. I hit it head on. Later, they said I was on the wrong side of the road.'

'Were you?'

'How the hell do I know? Maybe I was so high I drifted to the left, force of habit. Correction. I couldn't have been such a twit as that! Anyway, wham! Wasn't even time to hear the angels sing. Luckily, didn't kill anybody or I'd probably still be stuck in some filthy Spanish dungeon with the only key chucked down the drain. Driver got a few cuts, I gathered, later, but I was the one who copped it. Just as I deserved, of course. They never stopped telling me, you know? That was at a hospital a few miles out of Madrid. Gothic windows, church bells in the distance, nurses dressed like penguins and police . . . a relay team squatting on my bed, day and night, doodling in notebooks. I was there for six weeks, squinting through little slits in my bandages, on the look-out for a firing squad. All this time what was left of my face, the bit that wasn't glued to that coach bonnet like a mascot, was making the best of things without help from advanced science. A do-it-yourself moulding job. Not too hot, was it?'

For the first and only time Ted looked slightly uncomfortable. 'Look mate, surely somebody suggested . . .'

'A skin graft? I for one gave it a lot of thought. Not that I'm complaining, mind. I've no grouse at the hospital, they did their best. Changed the bandages twice a week, fed three liquid meals a day through another slit in my mask. Asked if I was a Catholic. Held my hand when I started screaming. But skin grafts cost a lot of pesetas, don't they? I'm probably being less than fair. Who could do anything with a mush like this? Bone structure smashed to hell . . . Consulate was helpful. Young bloke arrived, one day. Plummy accent. Pink shirt. Stood with his back to me looking out of the window. He knew his job, though. Got me off the hook in the end.'

'Shipped you home?'

'Ship? You're joking. Jet. Fast. Can you see a boat load of suburban bank clerks and their bronze birds offering me a game of deck tennis?'

'Another beer?' asked Ted.

'On me, this time,' said Keith. He dug out a pound note and pushed it across the table. Ted looked at it, long fair lashes dropping at last away from Keith's eyes, then suddenly back again. 'Suzuki a write-off?'

'Even the Japs must have cried! I got *some* insurance. Been meaning to buy another bike, but I haven't got my nerve back. For that – or anything else.'

Ted picked up Keith's pound note. 'Same again?'

'Ta.'

He vanished into the oasis of light crowded with elbows.

When he returned his shadow once again eclipsed the bar. He seemed unexpectedly at a loss. *Sorry, mate, I ought to have warned you .Why didn't you treat yourself to a double whisky?*

Ted's eyes were back over the frothy brim. 'I suppose you've got round to thinking ... that your face isn't the whole of you?'

'Great! Now we're getting round to the clichés.'

Ted grinned. 'Somebody described them as the copper coins of language. They jangle a bit, but you can't do without them.'

Keith said, 'Well, you might as well spend your loose change while you're about it. When are you going to tell me to pull my bloody socks up? When are you going to remind me about the people worse off than I am? Kids without arms and legs. Kids rotting with heroin or syphilis. Cripples. Mentally handicapped. Yeah, I know. Plenty of people worse off. When do we have the spiel ... about the noble human spirit triumphing over suffering? The guy with a cork leg who climbed the south face of Everest, the consumptive you read about who had two years to live so he started a leper colony in the Aleutian Islands.'

'Not much of a reader myself,' said Ted. 'Not much of a philosopher, either.'

'That's something in your favour!' Keith knew he was being aggressive now; needless, cruel aggro. He'd wanted to kick at somebody for a long time: enemy, friend, stranger – what was the difference? 'Well, now we've done the phoenix-out-of-the-ashes bit what's next?'

'You're doing the talking, remember?'

'Voluntary euthanasia. You've got a little book in the office, right? Full of addresses. Social services. Places where the homeless can kip down for a night, so long as they don't mind being kicked out the next morning – without breakfast. Marriage guidance. Pregnancy testing. Drug clinics. I can read even if you can't! There was an article about the Samaritans in *Titbits* last week.'

'No pictures with it!'

'Surely you've got a place on tap where they help suicides? Advice on how to do it, I mean, not a pep talk on rising above your misfortunes and collecting a prize for Zombie of the Year!'

'Zombie?'

The misshapen mouth trembled on the glass. 'All right, so I'm full of self-pity. You've got another little cliché in your pocket? Tell me I'll *get used to it*. Get used to people staring ... not going *on* staring, but fixing you with a fascinated gaze until you make the mistake of looking back. There's one exception ...'

'Yeah?'

'Got a short-sighted landlady and she's nice and dithery with it! A bit of luck I tell myself, and some day I'll meet this sexy blind bird. Be as well if she didn't have hands either, though, wouldn't it? Nice digs. Hot and cold, my own telly. Every day my landlady packs me sandwiches. That way I don't have to eat in the canteen. Yeah, I got a job. Are you beginning to wonder what I'm rabbiting on about? Store-keeper at the electronics factory, tucked away among the shelves of components at the back so I don't have to meet the customers. Or, rather, they don't have to meet me. The rest of my life ...'

'Shoot.'

'On a masochistic kick, are you, Ted? Luckily, there's a nightshift. Dark gates, skeleton staff – I'm hoping to keep the job. During the day, when I'm not asleep, my landlady lets me hang around. Her cat doesn't seem to mind. I just sit, watching the box. Open University, educational broadcasts, old movies, adverts for sunny holidays in Majorca ... soon as it gets dark I go out, as a rule. Like I did tonight. Back streets, mostly, and sometimes along the river. I go along the river and I think: I could jump off a bridge and nobody would care.

Always looks too bloody cold, though! There must be better ways, I think. Chucking myself in front of a train, stepping off a kerb in the path of a bus. Busting into a chemist and helping myself to some lethal pills. Never get round to it, though. Tell you something, Ted, or whatever your name is? I'm not the suicidal type. So why did I ring you?'

'The name really *is* Ted. You're scared you might do it after all? Like tonight . . .'

The slit of mouth twisted in wry self-mockery. 'Tonight? It was a mood, I guess. I was at my digs. The window was open a bit at the bottom. Unusual, that – perhaps my landlady's cat had wee-ed on the carpet or she'd spilt a bottle of carbolic. Anyway, I had this impulse to open it wider, take off head first. Then I thought: come off it, you clot, you're only one floor up. Suppose all you do is break your back and collect a new problem? But the mood kept going, you see? Even when I was out in the wet. I found myself making my way towards the river. The rain was dancing along the river and I remember standing on the bridge and feeling cold, cold right down inside. The water suddenly looked warm and deep and enclosing – like mummy's womb. Deep psychology, man! I started to climb the parapet.'

'And then?'

'A copper came along on a bike. It's not a crime any more, to do away with yourself, is it? Not that they ever could do much about it afterwards if you pulled it off. The copper gave me a sideways look as if he thought I was vandalizing an ancient ruin. He pedalled off across the bridge and kept looking back at me over his shoulder. Nearly fell off, silly bastard!'

'Then you rang us?'

'Not yet! The river looked cold again. I had a picture in my head of a corpse floating flat on its back – mine – maybe not being picked up for days. I didn't fancy my landlady being sent for to squint at my faceless corpse, trying to identify it. Poor old biddy deserves better. And there was something else . . .'

'Go on.'

'I hadn't written a note. Before you commit suicide, I thought, you write a note. Everybody else does. You need an audience, somebody to explain to, even if it's only a cub reporter chewing his pencil at the back of the coroner's court. It felt important . . .' Keith drained his glass, froth on his crinkled chin. 'That's about the lot, chum. Even you must have had enough. I'm due on the job in an hour. You know something? I've got three A-levels, good grades. I thought of studying medicine . . . before this happened.'

'And now?'

'Come off it, Ted. Suppose I got round to qualifying? I get behind some mortuary, doing autopsies. Or in a path. lab., glad that at least the rats look me in the face. Sorry, Ted – I'm wallowing.'

Ted suddenly looked very young – and very old. 'One wallow doesn't make a summer! And, although it's on your say so, you don't shake me as easily as that.'

'So come on, Jesus Christ Super Star, where's the miracle?'

'They take a bit longer, as the man said.'

'Another beer?' asked Keith.

'Next round is mine.'

'Forget it.' Keith evaded the eyes. He had some change left over from the pound note. He pushed it across the glass topped table. Ted looked at it thoughtfully. Fifty pence piece, two tens, a five, a couple of copper coins. Then his eyes came up again.

Once the mouth had belonged to a small boy; mischievous, pensive, defiant, sulky. Like any kid's mouth, changing from mood to mood. The mouth now, what was left of it, resembled a cleft in expressionless and random rock.

Then the voice said, without rancour, in desolation, 'You're a useless sod, Ted. Not your fault.'

Ted's eyes searched for Keith's over the empty glasses. 'You did say this was your round, mate?' He slowly, very slowly, pushed his glass across the table. 'So it's your bloody round, right? Thanks very much, I'll have another half pint.'

Keith picked up his money and turned towards the bar. The light across there under the beams glittered on glass and brass and faces. Faces! His fingers crept round the brim.

Out of his hate and fear and resentment gleamed, very faintly, a different light which was reborn of his own spirit.

Ted linked his fingers behind his neck, holding Keith in that same quizzical, unflinching gaze. 'Take-off point, mate. Your phrase.'

'You bastard!' said Keith.

And he collected the second glass and pushed his way to the bar.

The Edge of the Ceiling

ALAN GARNER

For the sick boy in this unusual story, there is first the discovery of
the Me within the physical self the world knows, and then the
discovery of how to get outside that physical self.

The idle fantasies of a bedridden child take him to an advanced
psychic state achieved by few people even in a lifetime of medi-
tation and 'out-of-body' techniques. Up and about on the ancient
Triassic cliff of Alderley Edge, he advances still farther, to 'switch
off' clock-bound Me and enter timeless space.

Mortally ill with meningitis, he hears himself dismissed as dead
by the doctors, and is angry enough to make himself live. 'I have
known my death ...' he says, 'but I have never felt so desperate
that I have wanted to die. I have felt so desperate that I have
wanted to live.' Triumphant affirmation of a survivor.

Despair can be powerful enough to kill you. It can also be
strong enough to force you back into life.

MONICA DICKENS

*

This is what happened.

Because nobody tells us, and because we have little experience, when we are children we accept as 'normal' whatever is
around us, although to an adult that 'normality' may be in-
tolerable and more than life is worth. So I can say honestly
that my own childhood was happy, and, unaware that children did not commonly live as I lived, I spent ten years in two
worlds.

The daily landscape for me was a bedroom ceiling in a
brick cottage. It was whitewashed, irregular plaster, steeply
pitched, with rafters and purlins and ridge exposed. And I lay

on my back beneath it through three long illnesses: diphtheria, meningitis and pneumonia.

I had no brothers or sisters: the Second World War came and went: the family survived. There were no tragedies. But the isolation caused by physical weakness and paralysis must have been increased by the more general isolation of a house threatened, bombed, blacked out.

When I was bedfast the rhythms of day and night were not imposed on me. Rather than sleep, I catnapped, or was in a coma.

Reality was the room.

The view from my window was for five years glued over with cheesecloth against bomb blast, but even unrestricted it was no more than a length of road on which little happened, and which was closed by the spire and weathercock of a Victorian church. Sideways rolling of my head made the spire wobble, the houses insecure and people on the road change shape. I knew that the uneven window-pane was the cause, but it still gave the room the reality. The ceiling did not wobble when I rolled my head.

There was a forest in the ceiling, with hills and clouds, and a road to the horizon. The way into the ceiling was harder for me at some times than at others. To enter it I had to stare at the road and remove detail from the sides of vision by slowly unfocusing my eyes. I had to block sound. I had to switch myself off.

'Switching off' is not a good description, because there was a total engagement in the activity of making the bed-bound 'Me' let go of me. The changes in sound and vision were felt by the 'Me' on the bed. I had to remove myself even from that.

I would concentrate on the concentration of the 'Me' concentrating. I thought of the thought of myself thinking. I observed the observer observing – until the observer was not the observed.

Whatever actually took place, the sensation was that of

sliding out of phase with the boy in the bed. And the automatic result was to find that I had crossed the neutralized zone from the bed into the ceiling.

I did not sleep. There was no relaxing of consciousness. It was the opposite. I had to think harder, relatively, than at any previous time of my life. The thoughts may have been unusual, but the thinking was not.

I could tell the difference between waking and sleeping because of something else that developed. It was the ability to program myself for dreaming before I slept, rather like choosing from a menu. Generally, the dreams would come in their programmed order, though nightmares were frequent and unsought. If I found myself in a nightmare I would first check that I was dreaming, then watch for the approach of the nightmare's particular horror and jump head-first into it to wake myself up.

I always knew when I was dreaming, because I could control the dream. The ceiling, however, I could not predict.

Once I was on the road in the ceiling, physically on it, there was no effort needed to keep me there. I entered, and did not look back. I did not see the boy on the bed. I felt that I was awake.

The world of the ceiling was three-dimensional, objects were solid, visual perspectives true. I never ate or drank in the ceiling. There was no wind, no climate, no heat, no cold, no time. The light came from no source and was shadowless, like neon. And everywhere, everybody, everything was white.

Another peculiarity was that I could see in the dark. If I lay in bed, in the black room, the ceiling was fluorescent-limned, or like a negative film. And when I went to the ceiling, the whole ceiling-world was lit by the same reversed light, and so were the people and so was I.

One quality that did seem remarkable at the time was the way in which sound behaved. Although voices moved about, their origin and focus, and therefore their transmitter, were

in me. It was the exact effect of listening to stereo sound on
headphones. It seemed remarkable, and has remained remarkable, because I had no precedent for the illusion and had to
wait another twenty-five years before I could hear it again.

Otherwise, the ceiling was, for me, natural. I met people I
knew, including my parents, and some who were only of the
ceiling. None of the 'ceiling people' has turned up in later life
yet, and they had no names. The people I knew in both states
of waking had no knowledge of the ceiling when I asked
them about it in the conventional world: but I soon stopped
asking.

Of course all this is interpretation now. I should not have
been able to describe the ceiling in these words at the age
when I lived there.

I lived in the ceiling, but there was a difference between
the ceiling and the bed that made the bed, with all its pain
and debility, the better permanent choice.

Although the way into the ceiling was along the same
road each time, the land beyond the road, from visit to visit,
was inconsistent, and this inconsistency made the ceiling not
more interesting but less so. Each venture was separate rather
than a process of learning, and such variety leads nowhere; it
builds nothing; it has nothing to teach. And I wanted to
learn. That was the difference. I would enter the ceiling by an
act of will, but I left it through boredom.

Sooner or later, I would stop whatever I was doing in the
ceiling, turn around, and always be facing the same
road–forest–cloud–hill picture. Then I would pull back, as a
camera does, to the bed and lie looking at the lime-washed
plaster.

There was one terror in the ceiling, one motionless threat.

Sometimes I would look up, and see no road, no forest,
clouds or hills, but a plump little old woman with a circular
face, hair parted down the middle and drawn to a tight bun,
lips pursed, and small, pebbled eyes. She sat wrapped in a

shawl in a cane wheelchair and watched me like a waning moon, her head turned to the side, as if she had broken her neck.

When I saw her, I knew that I could die. She must not enter the room, and I must not enter the ceiling. If I let her eyes blink, I should die.

There was no night, day, dawn, dusk. The little old woman and I were locked.

The little old woman came only when my life really was threatened. She was a part of the plaster in the ceiling, not of my room but of my parents', and I was taken there when I was too ill to be left alone. She was my death, and I knew it.

A hundred and fifty yards from bed, and behind the house, was my other world.

Later knowledge told me that it was an eroded fault-scarp, six hundred feet high, of the Keuper and Bunter Triassic Sandstones. To me, it was The Edge. A cliff covered with trees. When I was not confined to the house, I would spend my days and my nights on Alderley Edge.

The Edge is a Beauty Spot, but not beautiful. Geology and man have made it spectacular, but dangerous. The obvious danger is physical: a cliff that has been mined for copper and quarried for stone through centuries and then abandoned. It is easy to fall off its high rocks or down into its shafts. People get killed there. But those people are visitors. To be born to The Edge is to respect it.

Woodland, on a cliff of coloured stone, was just the beginning of that world for me.

My family is one of a hierarchy of craftsmen. In the best sense, we have always known our place. We worked it as miners and stonecutters. We culled its timber for houses and fuel, grew food on its soil.

At a deeper level, we accepted that King Arthur lay asleep behind a rock we called the Iron Gates. Our water supply was from the Holy Well, which granted wishes to tourists at weekends, and an income to the child of our family who, on a Monday morning, cleaned out the small change.

But for no money would that child have climbed the yew and the thorn that stood beside the well. And there was a memory that could hardly be restored to words – of how the well was not for wishing, but for the curing of barren women, and the offerings were of bent pins, not pence. And my own grandfather spoke of rags tied to the trees: but that had been a long time ago: he said.

So it is for a child born to The Edge. We knew our place, and knowledge passed beyond the material to the spiritual. I was brought up to respect both. They were there. Even the ghosts were of relatives.

Yet my relationship with that hill was different from that of the rest of my family. I was not the first to be intelligent, but I was the first to be educated: and as a result of gained knowledge, for me The Edge both stopped and melted time.

I knew enough geology to become amazed. I could trace a tidal vortex in the red, yellow, brown, blue, black, green strata; the print of water swirling for a second under the pull of wind and moon and held for two hundred million years. I felt the white pebbles in the rock, and wondered from what mountains they had come, by what river, and to what sea.

And in the fleeting I found the vision. In knowing the moment of the vortex, and of the pebble, which, if I could have watched for long enough, was not rock but liquid, I lost all sense of 'Me' upon the hill.

As with the ceiling, a barrier was down. But, perhaps because I was not weakened, fevered, paralysed, the result was different. I felt not that I entered a world, but that a world entered me.

There were no exploits such as the ceiling provided: no journeys: no people. Of the two landscapes the ceiling was the more mundane. But the ceiling had shown me that time was not simply a clock, and so I was open to the hill and to the metaphors of time that the hill gave.

The years of bed had developed another freedom.

For most children, I know now, time drags. That is because inertia is uncommon and days are filled with events. But where a child has only inertia, time must not rule. And I played with time as if it were chewing-gum, making a minute last an hour, and a day compress to a minute. I had to. If I had not kept time pliant, it would have set me like the pebble in the rock.

So I brought to the coloured hill and my strength the craft of the white ceiling and my weakness. I switched myself off. And the universe opened.

I was shown a totality of space and time. A kaleidoscope of images expanded so quickly that they fragmented. They were too many, too fast for individual detail or recall. They dropped below the subliminal threshold, but I felt the rip-tide of their surge, and the rip-tide has remained.

Yet, despite the hurly-burly beyond words, when I partook of the hill and the hill partook of me, there is a calm, which childhood could not give.

For if the child had been left with only a vision, if the 'Me' had not been replaced by a sense of true self, I do not know what would have happened. I do not know that I could have grown. With only a blind vision, I do not know that I could have survived.

That is what happened: but not all that happened.

I said at the beginning that, as children, we accept 'normality' to be whatever is around us, and I have tried to describe two experiences to demonstrate what I mean. Man, though, at every age, is also an animal with instincts that need no teaching, and the strongest instinct is for life. Yet in childhood, at three different times, I died.

It was not medical death in the way that it can now be defined. It was the opinion of doctors, humane men, around the bed of an organism under the rough ceiling of a cottage below Alderley Edge.

The child was technically alive, but all systems were about to collapse, and there was nothing more to be done with him. In one instance, meningitis, my mother was helped to accept the imminent death by being told that for me to recover would be a cruelty, because the damage to brain and spine would be massive, and I should be a bedridden thing for the rest of my life, not a person, not a son.

What those humane men did not take into account was that I was not yet dead. I could not signal, I was unable to communicate with the outside world, but I was not yet dead. I could hear. And I heard. I heard myself dismissed, written off. It was, to the animal in me, an attempt to kill my life.

I screamed, using no words, making no sound. The body was dying and nearly dead. But fury then was greater than death, and though nothing showed on the surface of the wasted creature under the sheet, inside was total war. I raged against everything in the cosmos. Inside me was worse than any zoo gone mad. Outside was calm, immobile, good as dead. And I think that that is why I lived. I was too angry to die.

I lived. For what?

The point is that mine was a glorious childhood. I would not wish it on anyone, nor on myself again. But it happened. And my good fortune was that I was able, as a child, to face the ultimate before experience tangled my brains.

I am not arguing for life-at-all-cost. I hope I am not so arrogant that I would even begin to tell other people in other circumstances what to do. Indeed, I am at a disadvantage. I have known my death and known its ways, but I have never felt so desperate that I have wanted to die. I have felt so desperate that I have wanted to live. I have pursued life through the Edge and the ceiling, through inner and outer space and time, and I am simply relating a number of connected events that, though personal to me, may by their dramatic simplicity be of some use, somewhere else, some day.

I speak as a survivor, and have described some techniques of survival which I used as a child. They were the instincts of an animal, but they went on to teach me something more.

They taught me that man transcends techniques and that all experience can be made positive and turned to good. But we can never afford to stop. If I had stopped, the technique of The Edge and the ceiling might have dwindled into a sloppy mysticism. But instead I endured the rigours of an education that matched vision with thought, each to feed the other, so that dreams and logic both had their place, both made sense, and legend and history could both be true.

In such a way one mere survival was transcended, and is to this day. Each connection seen brings greater awe. My privileged childhood integrated me by forcing me to choose whether to live or die, and from that integration I saw that inner and outer worlds did not collide but communicated, through my very being, their harmonies of poetry and prose. I saw a unity at work outside myself.

It comes to that decision. We must look at what we see, and make up our minds. The only way round is straight through. But that way is assured. If it were not, history would have removed us long ago, and I should not be writing, nor would there be anyone here to read.

Tommy

ANGELA IRENE STRATTON

The writer is fifteen. Already she has observed and understood more than many people have at fifty. She knows a lot about those spirit-killers, alienation and isolation. She understands the desolate belief that nobody else thinks or feels like you do. No hope of ever finding anyone.

Just reading this story makes your palms sweat. The confusion of self-consciousness is all too familiar. Of course, Tommy is longing to dance with the girl in the tight shimmering skirt. But of course when he gets the chance, he has to stammer, 'I hurt my foot.' And of course he cannot guess that the loud easy ways of the group at the dance may be covering the same kind of panic as his.

'Somebody must agree with him. Somebody must.' Walking in the night by the river, Tommy is as alone as if he were the last survivor of the holocaust.

MONICA DICKENS

*

The lights were too strong. Every inch of the room was brightly illuminated. Lights glared from each corner, from the walls, and from the ceiling, so that the floor was fretted by a hundred faint shadows. The only masking of their intensity came from the veil of smoke which swayed and undulated just below the ceiling. Beneath it, the dancers swung crazily to music they could not hear, for the juke-box in the corner, powerful though it was, was submerged under the curious music of conversation, the shrill soprano of the girls rising against the low, steady bass of the boys. They could not hear, but they danced, taking their rhythm from the record's insistent beat vibrating in the floor-boards. They twisted and writhed in solemn-faced ecstasy, and knew nothing.

Tommy braced himself against his chair, and winced. He settled back again, and watched through half-closed eyes the couple dancing in front of him. Everything was too much in this place, he thought slowly. The lights were too bright. The noise was too loud. The colours were too gay. And the people were too many. The people were much, much too many.

Bored, he looked around the room. The music had stopped, and the mesmerized dancers had drifted back to their seats. He began to study the people sitting opposite him. One boy had a girl sitting on his lap. He whispered something in her ear, and she giggled, pushing him away with one hand. The boy pulled her closer, and, glancing up, saw Tommy watching them. He winked, and turned back to the girl.

Embarrassed, Tommy looked away quickly. He looked straight into the eyes of a dark-haired girl standing near the juke-box. She was with three other girls, who were all talking together, each heedless of the other two, like three tape-recorders running simultaneously. They were apparently unaware of everybody outside their own group, but the girl stood slightly apart. She stared intently at Tommy, and her dark eyes were blank.

As he realized that she was watching him, Tommy instinctively put his hand to his cheek. He could feel the roughness of the scabs and pimples which disfigured his cheeks and forehead. There was a blush building up inside him. He sensed it, and tensed, every muscle of his body imploring it to stay hidden. Then came the hotness of his cheeks and neck, and the slipperiness of sweat on the hand that gripped the chair, and the wetness of it on his nose and upper lip. He stared hard at the floor, waiting for the blush to subside. He stared until the grain of the wood came to life and rushed across the floor in dizzy, zig-zag lines.

He lowered his hand, and put it into his pocket, and felt

the sixpence there. He suddenly longed to ask the girl to dance. He would stride easily across the dance-floor, and select his record. Then he would drop the sixpence in, and press the right buttons, and turn to the girl. 'Care to dance?' he would say. And she would glance across at her friends, and then nod and walk with him on to the floor. They would dance, engulfed by the hypnotic rhythm, and his hands would not sweat. When the music had finished, and they saw each other again, he would say, 'like something to drink?' and she would nod again. Then he would go across to the counter at the far end of the hall, and buy two soft drinks, and he would thread his way back through the groups of people, with a drink in each hand. He would give her one, and sit down beside her, and say, 'what's your name then?' And she would tell him, and then he would finish his drink and put the empty glass, beaded with moisture, on the ledge behind him, and he would ask her to dance again. And then – who knew what then? He had a sudden beautiful vision of himself and the girl lying in the long grass, with the warmth of the sun on their backs.

The desire to ask her to dance became unbearably strong. The sixpence seemed to swell in his hands, and to press against his fingers. There was a heavy knot of nervousness in his stomach; his legs were stiff against the floor.

He looked across at the girl. A tall, good-looking boy was standing in front of her. He spoke and she glanced at her friends and then nodded. Together they went on to the dance-floor, and waited for the needle to settle gently on the record.

Tommy felt suddenly empty. His eyes were smarting. He smiled cynically. 'I'd probably have pressed the wrong button on the juke-box, and lost my money,' he thought. He smiled again. 'She wasn't very good-looking anyway,' he philosophized, and inside he was empty with loneliness and disappointment.

He stood up abruptly, and stood before a window. The sky was black, and panting clouds rushed across it in grey wads. The moon seemed very high and pure, surrounded by a haze of fine silver. Tommy stared at it until he felt as if he were drowning in its whiteness. It filled his mind with its serenity, and exhausted his soul. Diana, goddess of the moon, he thought, and wondered suddenly where the thought had been hidden. He turned back to the crowded room, and hated it for not being as remote as the moon.

He sat down, and ran his fingers through his short, dark hair. For a second he looked at the dark-haired girl. He should have asked her to dance. Maybe it was still not too late. He could still ask her. She seemed to be a friendly girl. It was a bit stupid really, to come to a dance, and then not dance with anybody. What were the girls supposed to do? Ask him for a dance?

He looked up. A boy was standing in the door-way. He was small and fair, with quick, suspicious eyes, and a nervous tremor in the muscles of his neck. He looked round the room, and for a second, his eyes met Tommy. He turned around, to face the darkened hallway. Suddenly he was surrounded by others, four boys and several girls, gaily dressed and pretty-masked, with artificially dark eyes and high, toppling hair-styles. They were all dressed differently, and had different features, yet all looked the same, all models of the same proto-type. The boys were similar, too, big-shouldered and small-hipped with boy-tough faces and nervous hands.

The group looked around the room, much as the first boy had done. Moving together, they straightened and stiffened, and the boys flexed their nervous hands, and the girls wriggled their shoulders and patted their tall hair-pyramids, and looked at the boys' eyes. The boys glanced at each other, and stepped from the dim coldness of the hall into the eye-blinding, cheek-flushing gaiety of the dance-room.

They shrugged their way through the dancers, the girls

tripping behind on high heels, giggling and bristling coyly. One of the boys turned. 'Let's sit over there,' he suggested, indicating with an expansive circling of his arm the seats he meant.

Tommy felt a convulsive twisting deep in his stomach and at the base of his throat, as he realized that they intended to sit next to him. He slid along the bench, overwhelmed by a panicky determination not to be surrounded by this confident, compact group. He slid until his over-hot flesh flinched against the cold clamminess of the sudden wall. The boys stopped near him, and turned and hitched their trousers-legs and sat. The girls giggled, and collapsed between the boys, and beside the boys and on the boys. One of them oozed herself into a tiny space between Tommy and the boy next to him. She pressed her shoulders and arms against her boy-friend, and her thigh throbbed against Tommy's leg. Feeling the blush flaring within him again, Tommy pushed his whole body into the wall, and still her thigh burnt into his leg. Painfully aware of her tight, shimmering skirt closely following the curve of her knees, he looked along the side-wall. At the far end were some exposed bricks, irregular pink-browns, yellow-greys. He began to count them, and heard not the figures he thought, and did not even see the bricks. He heard only the girl's quick breathing and shrill laughter, and saw only her tight skirt, and felt the burning patch on his leg.

Suddenly, through the whirling, buzzing confusion of his thoughts, he heard the girl say, 'Do give over, Stevie, I'm pushing this kid through the wall here.'

The boy laughed. 'He don't mind. He's not complaining any, is he?'

Tommy turned to look at them, forcing himself to look into their eyes. The other boy grinned amicably. 'Hiyup?' he inquired.

Tommy fought to get his words past the dry agony of his

throat. 'Hello,' he answered, huskily, and hated the unpredictability of his breaking voice.

'I said, you don't mind me and my girl, do you?'

Tommy shook his head. 'No,' he answered.

The other boy shifted his position.

'Hard as hell, these benches,' he remarked.

Tommy nerved himself. 'They're specially made for strengthening your behinds.' A warm flood of pleasure saturated him. He could hold his own with anybody, he exulted.

'What's your name then, hey?'

'Thomas G – er, Tommy.'

'Uh-huh.' The boy had brown, hard eyes, and an exaggerated wave in his greased hair. He looked at Tommy for a second.

'I'm Stevie. Steven H. Lambert, to be exact.' He pronounced the 'aitch' with an aspirate. 'This is Les.'

Les smiled. 'Tommy,' she acknowledged him. Tommy nodded. He did not trust his voice.

'Haven't seen you around before?' The statement was a question.

'No, I don't get down this way much. Too much to do. Spend most of my time up-town,' Tommy lied desperately. This carelessly friendly girl with the green-lidded eyes and whitened lips, and this confident boy with an open smile and guarded eyes, they were not going to know that he spent most of his evenings laying on the sofa, gazing at the caged excitement of the cornered television.

'Uh-huh. Want to dance with Les?'

The question was so unexpected that all Tommy's reasoning powers left him. He blinked. 'With Les?' he repeated, for lack of something to say.

'Yes, sure. She don't mind who she dances with.'

One of the boys sitting further down the bench, overhearing, murmured to his neighbours, unsmiling until a roar of laughter assured him that his humour had been appreciated. Les leant forward. 'You shut up,' she said indignantly. 'Did you hear what he said, Stevie?' she demanded.

'I heard. You keep your mouth closed, Jim, while I'm around.' Stevie did not take his eyes off Tommy, who had lost the thread of the conversation. He thought over what had been said, and coloured as he realized why Les was so annoyed.

'Anyway, do you want to dance with Les?' Stevie asked.

'I don't think I can. I hurt my foot this morning. Coming down the stairs, it was. Caught my toe in a loose fold of the carpet.' Tommy longed to say, 'Sure. Why not?'

'Go on. No point in coming to a dance-hall, and then not dancing, is there?'

Les pushed him. 'Oh, do shut up, Stevie. You're embarrassing him. If he don't want to dance, he don't, and that's all there is to it. Don't you let him bully you, Tommy,' she added.

Tommy grinned. 'I won't,' he promised, and wanted to say, 'I guess it'll be all right, though. Come and dance.' He could. It would be quite easy. He was a reasonably good dancer. He formulated his speech. There would be no difficulty at all.

Les turned to Stevie. 'Are you going to sit here all night, or do we dance?' she demanded.

'Oh, come on then.' He winked at Tommy. 'Women!'

When they had left, Tommy sagged against the bench. He wondered why he had not asked Les to dance. He would have done so, if he had had a chance, he decided. He suddenly dreaded their return. He could not talk to them again. He stood up, and dried his sweating hands against his trousers, and combed his hair. Then he turned, shrugging on his coat, and edged his way between the benches and the mass of dancers.

Outside, the air was cold and moving. Tommy paused for a moment, grateful for the dark and the breeze and the silence. Behind him, he could hear the noise of the dance-hall, and the lights through the windows edged the lonely trees with gilt. He shivered, and thrust his hands deep into his trouser-pockets, digging his finger-nails into the dust in the seams. He hesitated, and then turned and walked away from the dance-hall.

The street was wonderfully deserted. Tommy walked quickly enjoying the sound of his heels striking the pavements, and the shadowing echo. The street was very long, so long that the end was hidden by walls of night. The pavements were grey, and circular-white in the cold light which grew from the ground, and converged upwards to the lamps which rose grotesquely along the kerb, stretching in graceless supplication to the secret skies.

Tommy turned up his coat-collar, and lowered his head. He wished the pavements were wet. He was a man in danger. Ahead of him, lay violence and death. He strode determinedly towards his fate, a lone man, independent of others. Tommy straightened his lips, and stared coolly at the black distance into which he was walking. Somewhere ahead, men awaited him, men of vengeance, men of hatred. No one stood by him, or for him. He needed no one. A gun was cold in his pocket.

A layer of dry leaves nearby coughed hoarsely. Tommy gasped, fear bursting upon his brain. Slowly, it subsided. Only a few old leaves. Tommy blinked, empty with relief. He quickened his step, his feet driving into the uneven cement, his legs aching. Above the mourning branches of the trees, the warm black sky quivered. The clouds had disappeared, leaving it flecked by a million, tremulous cigarette-ends, glowing through the fabric of the heavens. The moon was so very far away, and so incredibly clean. Tommy looked at it until his throat hurt with its loveliness. He consciously willed himself to be drawn into the vast solitariness of moon and space, fighting to conceive the inconceivable emptiness of time and place beyond his earth-rooted existence. This street, along which he walked, would never end. It wound on and on into the night, up and up through eternity to the chaste glory of the moon, and he alone walked it.

A laugh shattered his splendid loneliness, and all the hatred Tommy had ever known for sound and light and human existence tightened in his muscles. The road suddenly bored him. He turned into a tributary street, and ran fiercely down the long, winding slope. The railings and hedges blurred into a long, uneven multicoloured one, and the world was a bewildering rush of housenames: 'Thistbeds', 'Wanderer's Rest', 'Chez Nous', 'Dunroamin', 'Janine', – why Janine? Tommy's eyes pounded and his throat throbbed and his whole body jumped and bobbed; his heart strained painfully against his imprisoning flesh. At last his legs melted, and the pavement threw itself at him and tore his hands and knees, and flattened his life.

He lay for a still second where he had fallen. Then he got up, painfully and stiffly, rubbing his bruised knee. He limped slowly, heaving for breath. There was no sound, anywhere. Why Janine?

At the bottom of the road was the river. Tommy limped down the tired steps. At the bottom the secret water lisped softly against the stones. Tommy sat feeling the coldness through his trousers. He trailed his hand in the water, gazing across the river. It was black, much blacker than the sky above it. The filth and slime of the day was purged by the cleanliness of night. The water gurgled and slapped and bubbled a hundred thousand hidden messages, and Tommy heard them all. He watched where the tops of the waves glittered, and sensed the continuous movement he could not see. The water was quite bottomless. The mud, which Tommy knew was there by day, no longer existed. He wondered which would be more empty, sinking remorselessly downwards through the clinging, yielding water, or moving endlessly from a star to a star.

Across the river, the bank rose thick. The thin, straight, masculine lines of the motionless cranes towered above it, shaming the shapeless warehouses which crowded like old women, too often pregnant, at their feet. The soft, musky yellowness of the street-lamps filtered through the dark, and lay on the surface of the water, very different from the ice-sharp beams of the lamps along the long road.

Behind the cranes and warehouses straggled the senseless skyline of the city, rising and collapsing, jutting and sloping. Above it, the sky was reddened by street upon street of man-made lighting. Why, Tommy thought, did it look so attractive from across the water? He knew it was full of dirt and grime and pain, of sorrow and of lust, of disillusionment, of idealists about to become cynics, of dry-souled people so scared of the greatness of life and living that they shut their minds to the universe, and lived instead in a little synthetic world of football pools and champagne, baby napkins and theatres, stiletto heels and Tube trains, kitchen sinks and fluorescent lighting. A despicably narrow, little world, where you shut your mouth to keep your job, and broke your ideals to make your name, and yet – it looked so gay and warm from the darkness of the other side of the river.

A ship's hooter groaned weirdly up-river. Tommy wished he were on that ship. He would sail down the black, bottomless water, and out into the mad beauty of the green-depthed ocean, where the huge, full-bellied waves clambered over each other, and slid and crashed down, and heaved up again, studded with diamonds and capped with frothy ermine. Tommy had only been to sea once, but he had never forgotten the peace he had known, gazing into the waves, with the motion of the waves in his body and the noise of the waves in his ears, while the white stiff-winged sea-birds soared through the clear air, moaning plaintively.

That was what he would do. He would sail across the great ocean, and when he had stopped sailing, he would live alone, somewhere high so that the world was below him, and he was surrounded by nothing but the majestic solitude of the ancient mountains, topped by pure snow and clear ice, with the empty sky above. He would be free of the politics and the religions and the triviality of people. Nobody would tell him to get a job, or clean his shoes, or ban the bomb, or fill in a census form, or forget his principles, the ultimate sacrifice, it seemed, before success.

Tommy stared at the mucky water slopping at his feet. If only people were not necessary.

'Here, boy. Come here a minute.'

Tommy turned, and looked up the steps. A man, bulky in his overcoat, stood at the top, his hands in his pockets. Tommy scrambled up, and stood, uneasy, before him.

'I'm so sorry to disturb you.' His voice was low and smooth. 'Do you happen to know Grantham Road? We seem to be lost.'

'Certainly.' Tommy attempted to imitate the man's cultured speaking. He swung round, one arm outstretched. For the first time, he noticed the two women in the shadows. The elder was bulky, like the man, and well-dressed and annoyed; she twitched impatiently. The other was a girl. He could hardly see her, just her eyes, and the creamy warmth of fur at her neck. Tommy flushed in the darkness, embarrassed by her presence. He turned back to the man.

'Go along that street over there and turn into Rolins Avenue, that's the second on the right: then turn left, and go down Johns Street, and Grantham Road is the third one along on the right-'and side.'

Tommy felt sick as he heard the mispronounced 'hand'. He turned away as the man thanked him, and stood at the top of the steps, leaning on the cold parapet, and listening to the man's heavy footsteps, interspersed by the light chatter of women's heels.

Why did people always have to spoil everything? Why did

it matter if he forgot an 'h'? But it did matter. He knew it mattered, and the knowledge increased the hatred. He hated having to live by standards he judged to be false, having to be careful that what he said never offended, angered or shocked his hearer, that he never did anything which others might feel was wrong. He hated having to pray to a God he neither understood nor found fully credible. He hated humanity, with its class distinctions and prejudice and stupidity, its terrible, blind, mass stupidity.

Tommy pressed his hands against the impassive stones, and listened to the wailing, disembodied ship's siren. The shadows stirred slightly in the corner of his vision. He turned, relaxing his taut body, and watched the long, lean cat slide across the ground. It was black, blacker than the night, and its sleek fur gleamed like the water. The intense, golden eyes burnt warily, and the easy-moving body rippled with every silent step. The cat's head was high.

Tommy sighed, a low, shuddering sigh. What a beautiful creature, he thought, and the adjective was pitifully inadequate when applied to the aloof, regal, mystical, loveliness of the cat. He sank to one knee, holding out his hand to it, terrified lest it should be frightened.

The cat regarded him, unblinking. In one fluid movement it was beside him, chafing warmly against his cold palms. Tommy stood up, clutching it against him, and set it on the parapet. He stroked its wiry fur, and looked, fascinated into its eyes. Like two lonely moons. The Egyptians had held the cat to be sacred, he remembered, and silently commended them. It was the goddess of loneliness.

The cat was suddenly gone. It jumped soundlessly to the ground, landing four-footed, and padded away into the night. Tommy watched it go, the rasp of its fur still on his hand, and saw the plump, thick-furred, grey cat which was unexpectedly beside the black cat.

Tommy turned back to the river. The cat was joined. From

out of the dark air, a grey ship swished through the water. It looked huge and irresistible, carving through the melting waves.

A laugh crashed through the whisperings of the river, and a cabin-light leaped into life. Tommy could see the peak-capped officer who stood on the bridge. He moved his arm, and a second later, the siren sounded.

Only the moon was lonely, then? The town was bursting and bulging with gregarious life. The river merely slumbered. Only the moon – and himself.

But how could one person be utterly alone? Surely his emotions and ideas, his desire and his rebellion, surely they were not peculiar to him. Men before him must have felt as he did. And in the present world, among those millions of life, others must be groping and fighting for the same things as he was. One brain could not be entirely original. Somebody must agree with him. Somebody must.

But no one was here. Not on the river-banks, in the night. There was no one but Tommy on the river-bank.

Tommy turned, pushing his hands into his dusty pockets, hunching his shoulders against the breeze. He walked up the slope of the long, coiling road, past the house called 'Janine', away from the secretive water.

He walked. The silent moon moved, bird-like, through the night-sky. Lights flashed, died, flickered. The ship swept down to the ocean. Loud music floated starwards. A hundred thousand youngsters danced heedlessly. And Tommy walked. He walked back.

Teenage Suicide

JEREMY SEABROOK

What makes people want to kill themselves when they are young? When they make suicide attempts, do they really want to die?

There are as many reasons as there are unhappy people. Here are the stories of four of them, in their own words.

The despair that can lead to a suicide attempt comes through, but so does hope, and the industructible spark of the survival.

Listen to Tessa, after a near-fatal overdose: 'That was the point at which I decided I really wanted to live; you have to go as close as that to death before you realize what a gift life is.'

MONICA DICKENS

*

It is especially difficult to talk to young people who feel suicidally unhappy: if they could talk about how they feel, this would be a considerable step towards solving the problem. It is precisely because they cannot be reached that there is such concern. What I have tried to do is talk to young people who successfully lived through their moment of darkness and despair. Their experience seems to me not so very different from that of many who feel that no one could possibly understand what they are going through. But the most important thing to remember is that we are not alone: our isolation, our despair, our shame are not really our own at all, but are an experience which all humanity shares.

In our society, children have to carry a peculiar burden, which is not officially recognized. Children and young people have always been a source of hope to the old, symbols of continuity, and a consolation to parents and grandparents for the fact that they have to grow old. But now, young people have an additional role, which it is sometimes hard to bear. Although children have always meant hope and the future, the values which they have carried have always, in the past, been given to them by their parents. Their role has been to carry on traditional wisdom, the ideas and beliefs of the past. But with the breakdown of traditional parent/children relationships, young people are left with the burden of having to provide a meaning for life for their own parents, a reason for living. Where it has always been the parents who told their children what to believe and what to think, it is now the parents who expect the children to conjure a meaning for them out of thin air.

Now this is an impossible task.

A generation is now growing up who have been given the best of everything. How many parents do you hear say, 'You've had the best money could buy'; 'Nothing's been too good for them'; 'I worshipped that child'; 'He's had everything he wanted.' And the unspoken transaction that has occurred between parents and children has been this: 'I will give you everything, and you will give me the reward of being exactly as I want you to be.'

Children have been given everything: prizes, rewards, presents, gifts, treats. They have been endlessly affirmed and rewarded; but nothing has been asked of them in return: nothing has challenged them. They have been shielded and protected. They have been born to a society that kindles appetites rather than abilities: wants and needs rather than what they can achieve. In a society where people are measured by what they can get and have, and not by what they can make or create, the children can only suffer in the end. Children have been reared to expect constant happiness; an endless flow of things. They have been shielded from suffering; if things go wrong, they are invited to flee into fantasy and escapism. They have been sheltered from reality. Childhood is for us now a time of repression: repression of resourcefulness, initiative and imagination, and the replacement of these things by the development of needs, wants and appetites. And it is through these things that he seeks fulfilment in vain. So when he lives through the moments of despair and depression, anxiety, inferiority, shame, guilt, he is overwhelmed by them, because he has never had to face them, never even been led to believe that such things exist. The adult world, with the best intentions, seeks to shield children, and in doing so, cuts them off from a large part of reality: the negative and unhappy and inadequate feelings that exist side by side with the positive ones, and without which joy and happiness and laughter would have no meaning.

I spoke with four young people, all of whom thought they were unique in their own suffering. They all survived; but the simple recognition that they were not alone in their experience could have saved a great deal of unhappiness.

Kevin is sixteen. He left school in July 1977, and had a job in a supermarket that lasted two months; since then he has not worked.

'I don't know what's the matter with me. I feel as though everybody else is better off than I am. I don't mean money, although that would help. Everybody seems to know who they are and what they want, I don't know if you know what I mean. My old man don't talk to me, except to tell me how useless I am. He tells me I can't do anything, I've got no brains. They both tell me all the time all they've done for me, and I just don't see it. I can't do anything, I'm not very clever, I can't keep a girlfriend, I'm not good-looking . . . so what did they do for me? I used to go about with a gang, and we had girlfriends, but I never know what to say to them. If I get on my own with her, I've got nothing to say. If I go out with them once, they don't want to see me again. I get so lonely. I've got mates, kids I knock around with, but all they want to do is smash things up, nick things, sniff glue. They talk about football, I'm not interested. I wish I was. I'm not interested in anything else either. I'm deaf in my right ear, I don't even like discos. What I do, I like to imagine I'm somebody else all the time. I think I might be a hero. I wish there was a war. I wouldn't mind getting killed. I'd like to be a pilot of a plane. I hate me, and where I live and what I do. I spend most of the morning in bed, I had a job in a big store, but I hated it. I was just piling things up and pushing them round the supermarket. It was boring. I think I spend most of my time being bored. I can't see any point in doing anything. That's why I thought about dying a lot. If I was dead, I might know the reason why I was born. I believe there's life after death. I think you might come back as something else. A bird, or a horse or a tiger ... Sometimes I think I'd like to achieve something. Eddie Kidd, that's somebody I could admire. I had a motorbike, only it got vandalized ... Eddie Kidd, his life has some purpose to it. But what am I for?

'My Mum and Dad are all right. He's not my real father. All they do is watch television. He's got a milk round, she works in a factory. They just sit there. We live in a flat, it's half a house really. I hate it. Nobody round there is alive anyway, it wouldn't make much difference if they all died. What I'd do, I'd jump in front of a train if I wanted to do anything ... I can just see it. "He was ever so quiet. We never knew anything was wrong." '

Tessa, now twenty: 'I was the oldest of three children. I went to a good school in Surrey, and my father worked for a multinational company. I was clever, and he had an academic career mapped out for me. His job took him to New Zealand when I was sixteen; and there was something about the uprooting at that time that just disturbed me. The school I went to in Auckland was horrible – grey gloves in winter, white gloves in summer sort of mentality. It was unbelievably narrow and conformist. I discovered that my education in England had put me far ahead of the others I was with. In England I'd been quite a good participating member of the school, but there I was an instant outsider. I used to stay away from lessons, and I flouted the rules, and the only reason I didn't get expelled was that I'd only two terms to go before doing university entrance: my A levels that I'd got in England were more than adequate for what was expected of me there. The people I gravitated towards were those few, pitifully few, who didn't conform. Naturally at that time, we tended to take LSD. I took it several times, and although I'd had one or two bad trips, on the whole I'd enjoyed it. Well, I had a really bad trip; and this time it was indescribable. It started off all right; I travelled through space and time, I went through the galaxies, experienced the incredible vividness of things, sensory experience, the extension and contraction of space, the sound of things, the colours ... I became aware of the non-existence of time; it was as though I 'had transcended my self, I'd really achieved the ultimate escape. The only thing was, it didn't stop. Fortunately I had some good friends with me. They dosed me with sleeping tablets, but they had no effect. I didn't come down at all. They phoned my parents and told them we were going out of town for a time, and we went to Adelaide. For a fortnight I was completely freaked out. I didn't speak a single word all that time, I couldn't. I couldn't do a thing for myself, I couldn't wash myself or feed myself. They had to feed me and care for me, I was helpless as a baby. I could scarcely remember who I was. When eventually I began to come down, everything was wrong somehow. The familiar objects, things I knew perfectly well, somehow wouldn't fit into my perceptions. I looked at a chair and I had to say to myself, 'That's a chair, you sit on that,' 'That's a table,' 'That's a book, I know what you do with books, you read them.' I had to tell myself what everything was, in the most basic way. I had the feeling that I'd visited a different reality; but the awful indescribable thing was that the one I'd come back to was not the one I'd left. Only nobody seemed to understand, you couldn't describe it to anyone. You couldn't communicate – no one had had the experience; you felt terribly alone.

'It was partly as a result of that experience that I started on heroin, and I became a heroin addict for three years. The boy I was with at the time was on heroin, and it was really to help me get over that traumatic trip that he suggested I should try it, to help me slow down. Heroin acts as a block on your perceptions, everything comes in so slowly and gently, the idea was that it might counteract some of the effects of the over-active trip. The point about getting addicted is that you don't realize it's happening. You think, 'Well I'll try it once,' and then 'I think I'll do it again this weekend.' You don't doubt that you're in control. Then you say to yourself you'll do it once a week, and the fact that you do it only at weekends reassures you that you're only doing it for pleasure. The way I found out I was addicted was that I'd got ten capsules one weekend, and I sold them all, and was left without any. And I felt this sense of desperation, suddenly. That was how I realized. It wasn't that I had withdrawal symptoms, it was just that I needed it increasingly just to perform as a normal human being. Your equilibrium depends on having access to a regular dose.

'Through all this I started at the university, and I was still able to do a certain amount of work. While I was still in the after-effects of the bad trip, I went to Student Health to see the doctor. I tried to explain to him that the reality I was in then was not the reality I had originally left; and he said to me something like "Describe how it feels", and I thought he'd said that he understood what I'd been trying to tell everyone else, something they couldn't or didn't want to understand;

and I started to spill it all out, all the things I'd tried to explain; it must have sounded absolutely demented, because he looked at me as though I were crazy; which in fact I was. I use the word deliberately. I literally went crazy. For months it was as though there was a slowly thickening wall of glass between myself and other people. Communication seemed hopeless, impossible. I felt I was being more and more cut off from other people and the world they lived in. Incredibly, I went to do my exams. I didn't think I'd be able to do any of them, but somehow I did; all but one. That was chemistry. I was given some graph paper, and instead of writing the answers, I just looked at the paper, and couldn't imagine what it was for. I looked at all the little squares, and thought it must be to write a letter. So I spent the whole time writing this letter to someone I knew, and when they came to collect the papers, I thought the woman who was invigilating was going to post it for me.

'The life you lead as an addict is very degrading. In the end, you need so much of the stuff that getting it becomes the main occupation of your life. That generally means getting the money. If you're a man, there are two ways – either you deal or you steal. If you're a woman, there was stealing or the massage parlour. I couldn't quite face prostitution, so I went for stealing. My boyfriend had a gun; that's what it does to you, you'll shoot, you'll do anything to get the money. I can't tell you what squalor I lived through. Once, when I was doing an exam, I had to get a fix before I went into the examination room, and I was a bit careless, I used a hypodermic that was dirty. Within a few hours I was in hospital with a raging fever and sepsis of the blood. You degenerate terribly. It was at the worst time of my addiction that I did try suicide. I took a lot of tablets. I thought I'd finish with it, and I nearly succeeded. Through the burning fog of my perceptions I actually overheard some of the doctors talking about me. One of them said, "Well, she's a gonner. I hope they've sent for her parents, because she won't last more than a few hours." I realized that they were talking about me. I couldn't bear to think that I was being cast aside just like a lump of useless meat. I felt a tremendous anger inside me; and that was what gave me the will to live. From somewhere, I found this energy to live. I vowed I would pull through somehow, I couldn't bear the futility of ending up like that.

'And in fact, I did. They had actually prepared a bed for me in the hospital, because they were convinced that if I did survive, I would be little more than a vegetable ... Anyway, that was the point at which I decided I really wanted to live; you have to go as close as that to death before you realize what a gift life is.

'I managed to get myself together sufficiently to want to kick the habit. It was so painful; excruciating. The third and fourth days are the worst; and you feel like death on the first day; sickness and vomiting, being first hot then cold, sweating and trembling. At that time I weighed less than seven stone. I was neglected and half starved. I saw a lot of my friends die, others reduced to a shadow of humanity.

'Since then I've worked in a mental hospital for a year. I think I understand people better now. I want to work with people in some humanitarian way. I think I've probably something positive to offer. However bad you feel, nothing is worth getting involved with self-destruction like I was. To breathe freely again, no longer to be addicted, I feel I've been born again. Nothing is worth losing contact with reality for; however unbearable reality seems, it's millions of times better than what you put in its place. Whatever unhappiness, whatever loss or loneliness, it can't compare with the utter despair of an experience like that.'

Tina, now nineteen: 'I was married when I was seventeen;

by eighteen I'd tried to kill myself twice. I'm nineteen now. I haven't seen him for a year, and I hope I never see him again.

'I still feel I don't know what hit me. I was at school, and I hated it. I didn't like anything they taught us, I wasn't interested. I didn't go very much in the last couple of years. My mate Carole, her Mum was working, and her flat was empty all day. We used to go up there a lot with some boys. We spent one winter up there almost every day, drinking and mucking about, listening to music and that. We had some good times, I didn't regret it. I fell for this boy Steve, and I was only fifteen when we got engaged, secret engagement, you know, but then he went off with my mate and I felt so rotten, I went to live with Terry who was twenty-seven. His wife had left him. That was terrible, he wanted me to be a bleeding housewife, and I was sixteen. He worked on the buildings, and when he came home, he just wanted to sit and watch telly all night. So I used to go out on my own. One day he followed me to this disco and beat me up because I was dancing with some boy. Then I went back home for a little while, and my Dad wouldn't speak to me, he called me all the filthy slags under the sun. I just met Lorrie one night in a pub, and then three weeks later we just got married. It was terrible. There was my Mum and his Mum sitting in the register office, asking each other what their first names were. It was more like a funeral, dead right it was. I mean, I think it's right to take a chance in life, you have to. I know people who've known each other years before they get married and they're miserable as hell; and others I know who only had a sort of whirlwind romance, and they're on cloud seven all the time.

'So we went to live in this flat. After the wedding reception, in the evening we just went home. It was horrible. I felt lonely when we got home. He was moody, I don't know. There was something wrong with him, he'd got no mother or father, well his mother had left him in care and gone back to

Liverpool. He was cruel. It was his delight to torment me. He used to talk about murders and violence, terrible tortures that had happened, what people did to each other. He frightened me. I thought at first I'd married a maniac. Then he could be so lovely and gentle, it was like being with another person. But he was jealous of me, swore I was meeting other blokes in the daytime when he was at work. He used to follow me, or get his mates to follow. Some nights he used to lock me in the flat, and said he was going to set fire to it ... He used to go with other girls, and sometimes he brought them back to the flat, and he even used to get into bed with them while I was in the next room ... That was when I cut my wrists the first time, I've still got the scars. Then things were all right again for a little while, and he said he was sorry, how much he loved me; but he wanted to make me suffer. He didn't know why, and he said he wouldn't do it again. But he did. And then I got pregnant and Stacy was born, and I tried to kill myself then, because he said he'd gone off me when I was pregnant, and he thought I was repulsive and ugly and then I tried to kill myself. I took an overdose and I had Stacy taken away because I hated her, because I thought it was her fault that had made Lorrie go away, and I couldn't trust myself what I might do to her ... So I told my social worker, and they took her away. But I miss her, I've got nobody at the moment.

'I didn't think life would be like that. Nobody told me a thing. I knew about sex, everybody knows about sex. It's people you don't know about. Why is it, I sit and ask myself all the while, people can be so cruel and terrible to each other, even the ones that they love? That's the big mystery. Nobody told me about that. I feel I was conned. I was conned. I don't know who by. If I did I'd kill 'em.'

Roy, sixteen: 'Both my mother and father had been married before, and I was the second child of their second marriage. I was always a weak child, and I was a bit undersized. Even at Primary School I was called a cissy, because I preferred doing things girls do rather than boys; and I was always playing with girls.

'My parents didn't get on. The trouble was that they both chose me to complain to about each other. My brother was much more independent than I was. We never got on very well. My mother kept telling me about her first husband, what a good man he was, and she should never have married my father. She used to say he would drive her mad, and one day she went out and threw herself in the river. I don't think she was really serious about killing herself, because it was summer and the river was very low anyway; but she was always threatening to run away, to do herself in; it made me very insecure. She used to say it was only the children that stopped her from killing herself, but that made it worse, because it made you feel that you had to make life worthwhile for her, because it was on my account she wasn't killing herself. My father's reaction to this was to sneer at me, because I always took her part; and he used to say I was a Mummy's boy and a weakling, and that I'd never amount to anything, and I'd better learn to hold a brush because I'd never do anything more than sweep the roads.

'I went to a comprehensive school, and I got teased and bullied because I was such an easy target. And I used to cry very easily, and they loved that. I knew all about homosexuality, and I used to join in all the jokes about pouffs and fairies and all that; then when I was fourteen, I went to the cinema and met a bloke there and we masturbated each other. I went home and I was so overwhelmed by what I'd done, I vowed I'd never never give expression to my homosexuality again. And for a few months I managed to keep myself in control; but in the end I deliberately went round the toilets where I knew men used to go, and I went with a man, and afterwards I felt desperate. I thought I'd rather die than be a queer, so I decided I'd finish my life. I felt worthless and useless and ugly. I thought the only thing would be to kill myself. I'd got it all worked out. What I was going to do, I was going up to this tower block near where we lived, and I was going to jump off. All the balconies at the top, there was a sort of opening and there was a sheer drop of eighteen stories. I'd even decided a day when I'd do it. And when I'd made up my mind that there was a way out, I felt ever so happy. I thought, "Well, that's the solution to all my problems, I needn't worry any more." And for the first time I can honestly say I felt really good. In fact, I'd got one friend at school, he was a bit like me, we didn't get on very well with the other kids, we weren't very keen on football; and that night I went round his house, and I thought I'd tell him what I was going to do. So I did. And I told him why. And he said he felt the same way, because he felt he was attracted to men all the time. He said even when he walked down the street, he used to fancy all the men he saw. Well I was lucky. That was such a relief. I felt I wasn't alone, and he felt the same. It made all my plans seem a bit ridiculous. We've had some laughs over it since. I can't say I'm happy being like this; but I don't think there's anything wrong with it. I'd prefer to be in the majority, but that's it. In fact, I made the mistake of telling my mother after I'd told Stephen, and that was a disaster. She wanted to cart me off to psychiatrists and get me cured, and I told her that it was hopeless. Nothing ever came of it fortunately, but she watches me like a hawk, and it gave my father some justification for hating me. I still live at home. I'm doing A levels, but I can't wait for the time when I can get away, leave the town and go and be independent. I feel life has got a lot to offer me, and I'd hate to think I missed any of it by doing anything as negative and futile as committing suicide.'

The Aggie Match
LYNNE REID BANKS

Loneliness here is not because of loss, or the failure to reach out and be reached. It is because of circumstance. Ronnie has simply always been alone with his silent parents on the Canadian farm a hundred miles from town, and he is eight before he fully discovers how other children play and fight and compete, and what friendship is. That discovery is going to leave him lonelier than ever for a time, back on the empty farm. You don't really miss something till you've had it. But he will find it again.

'Who was that, anyway?' his father asks in the truck going home.

'My friend,' Ronnie answers. He has made his breakthrough.

MONICA DICKENS

＊

Ronnie was a lonely little boy. He lived with his father and mother on a farm in Canada. He had no brothers or sisters, and no friends either, because the farm was far away from everywhere.

When he looked out of his bedroom window, or any other window of the wooden farm house, all he could see was miles and miles and miles of flat wheat-fields. Sometimes they were covered with green or golden wheat, which rippled in the wind like the waves of the sea. In autumn there was only stubble, which made Ronnie feel sad because it looked so dead and finished. In the winter deep snow fell, and then Ronnie's window-world was white, white, white, and flat as far as he could see.

A long straight road ran past Ronnie's house. It came from

far away in one direction, got wider and wider till it came to the farm; then it started to get narrower again as it stretched away towards the far-off horizon. There it came to a point and disappeared. It was a very dull road, with never a bend in it, and nothing on either side but the wheat-fields, and telegraph poles. But Ronnie always began each day by running to the window of his bedroom and looking along it one way, then running out, across the corridor at the top of the wooden stairs and into his mother's and father's room, to look along it the other way.

And sometimes – not very often – he would see a car or a truck somewhere along those empty miles of road. He would hang out of the window, watching the moving speck get nearer and nearer; when it passed one special telegraph pole he knew he must rush down the stairs and out of doors to be by the roadside when it went roaring past. And afterwards he ran up the stairs again to hang out of the window on the other side of the house and watch the car or truck become a tiny speck again. He liked these times very much, but he always felt depressed after them.

Ronnie was nearly eight. For a long time now, his mother had been talking about him going to school. Ronnie wanted to go to school more than he wanted anything in the world, more than a bicycle or even a pony. At school would be other children. At school there would be lots of noise.

Ronnie didn't hate living on the farm; it was all he knew. But he hated the quiet. He used to stand outdoors and listen for sounds. There was the singing of birds, and the sound of his father's tractor sometimes, or, if he stood by the kitchen window, the sounds his mother made, filling the stove with cut wood or bumping the legs of the table with the broom or clicking the wooden spoon against the sides of the bowl when she was making cake. They were all nice sounds, but there were not nearly enough of them.

The sound of people's voices was what Ronnie wanted most.

His father and mother were very nearly the only people Ronnie ever saw, or heard. And they were both very quiet. When his father came in at night after work, he was tired. He didn't talk much. His mother talked sometimes, but she, too, was always very busy. Sometimes when Ronnie wanted to talk he would go into the kitchen and stand by the door and stare at her and hope she would speak to him. Sometimes she noticed him and said something, but it was usually something like 'Is anything wrong? Why don't you play outside?' Then she would probably give him a cookie and shoo him out again because he was in her way.

Often he said to her, 'When will I go to school, Mother?'

And she'd say, 'When we find a way to take you.'

Ronnie understood this problem. The school was in Town, and Town was a hundred miles away. How could a person's father, who anyway had to get up at dawn to do his work, find time to drive a person a hundred miles to school?

Going into Town in the farm truck was something they did once a month. It was the greatest thing in Ronnie's life. He counted the days, starting with the day after a visit, and because of this he could count backwards from thirty before he could count forwards.

'How many days left now, Mother?'

'Twenty-nine – twenty-eight – twenty-seven – twenty-six . . .' all the way down to 'One more. Tomorrow we're going.'

On one-more nights, Ronnie couldn't sleep, at least not till late, going to Town was so exciting. There was the general store, where his mother handed in a long list of supplies and the man piled the huge bags of flour and sugar and potatoes and the tins of jam and the big dried-up-looking chunks of meat into an enormous box which his father put into the back of the truck. And there was the street full of people and cars and bicycles and trucks, and sometimes horses. And the railway station with its trains and the big grain-elevators standing up against the sky.

And the people! Lots and lots of them, all talking and laughing and shouting and making lovely, peopley noises. There were children too, though Ronnie was too shy to speak to any of them. He just liked to stand near his mother as she shopped, or hang around outside and watch them running and playing.

They seemed to know how to play in a way that he didn't. For one thing, they had toys. Ronnie had very few toys. He had an old skipping-rope that he couldn't skip with, although he knew a lot of other things to do with it; and a cardboard boat that his mother had made him from one of the store-boxes, with two sticks for oars; and a football, though that had burst and wasn't much good; and an old hobby-horse that his father had made him long ago. He also had a lot of bits and pieces that nobody else wanted, like a worn-out tractor tyre, and some broken dishes, and a bent spoon for digging and an old hammer for hammering nails, and some empty paint-tins, and a length of chain, and some other things like that.

But his favourite toy was a glass marble. He'd found it one day in the street of the Town, and his mother had said he could keep it.

As soon as the first real mud of the big thaw had begun to dry, leaving patches of dark bare earth, the boys of the Town and some girls too would crouch round a little hole they made with a stick. They took their marbles ('aggies' they called them) out of little bags, and tried to knock them into the hole with crooked forefingers. There were many rules and words connected with the game, which Ronnie, watching from a safe distance, was beginning to master.

He knew that you could, if you were clever, win aggies from other children – that some children went home with bulging bags and others, sadly, with flat empty ones. He had seen one little boy cry because he had lost all his aggies. But then he had run to his mother, who was in the store with Ronnie's own mother, buying things, and she had at once bought him a whole new bag of aggies and he had joined in the game again.

Such incidents puzzled Ronnie. Why had some people a lot of money and others, like his family, so little? Why did some people live in Town and go to school and have friends, or even brothers and sisters, and people like himself live far away out on the prairie? Why, come to that, did some children have chatty, gossiping, laughing mothers, and hearty fathers who slapped each other on the back and got red faces and louder voices in the town Bar, when his mother and father were so silent and serious?

But one question worried Ronnie more than these. Other children could talk and laugh together, run up to each other and say, 'Let's play!' One boy could give another boy a push so they rolled over together, fighting and struggling, and then they were friends afterwards. How could they open their mouths and shout and yell, and throw their bodies about without worrying about getting hurt or dirty? Why did they seem so free, when he felt so shut-in?

He would stand in the street, always close to a building or a car so that he didn't feel too exposed, and preferably in the shadows, and watch them, and wish he were like them. Even when their mothers called them and they were rude, or took no notice, or ran away to play round a corner – even when a mother or father, infuriated, would give chase and drag a child back, scolding or shaking him, shouting at him for getting his clothes muddy or being disobedient – even then, Ronnie envied them. When his own mother or father called, he always ran at once – he meant not to, he meant to be naughty like the others, but his body obeyed before he had time to tell it not to. He was used to obeying.

One Town-day he was standing silently watching an aggie-match. It was taking place in a patch of spring sunshine beside the wooden store-building. There was a vacant lot there, with bushes and tall grasses, where Ronnie had watched the children playing hide-and-seek and other more complicated games, but near the building was a patch of earth on a little rise which always dried out early. This was always the first aggie-ground to come into use each year, and there was usually a fight for first rights to it.

The game was getting very exciting. Only three boys were left with any marbles. Two of them had won away from the others all they had. Now the third of the boys had only two aggies left, and they were both his beauties; he said he never played with them because he didn't want to risk losing them.

Ronnie was close enough to see them, in fact he was quite familiar with them because he had seen this boy take them out of his pocket and look at them lovingly. One was a large, dark blue one with something like a flower inside. But the other was the best. It was a pale yellow, no, not quite yellow, sort of gold – Ronnie could not think of anything he knew which was exactly the same colour, except perhaps the wheat when it first lost its green, before it turned that hard straw-yellow. It was plain glass except for a scattering of tiny, tiny bubbles inside, and it was perfect, no scratches or chips like the 'working' aggies soon got when they were much played with. Ronnie saw the boy who owned this treasure holding it up to the light and gazing at it with the same wonder as he felt himself. The other two boys waited, pretending scorn but actually with the light of greed in their eyes.

'Aw, g'wan – play it! What use is an aggie if you never play it?'

'Only girls keep the pretty ones and don't chance 'em!'

'It'll get scratched,' said the third boy.

'Maybe you'll get it straight in. Maybe it'll be a lucky one for you, and you'll win our two and won't have to play your goldie any more.'

'Anyways, if you don't play it, you're out of the game.'

The boy made his decision.

'I'll play my bluey first. But you two gotta play your beauties too.'

'Okay!'

The group of players who had fallen out crowded round to watch. Their grime-backed forefingers, with which they had been shooting the aggies, twitched in sympathy as the boy spat on his bluey and rubbed it on his sleeve for luck. The three players stood with toes on a scratched line, and at the signal they threw their aggies towards the hole.

Ronnie moved nearer. He had to, or he couldn't see. He crouched behind the line of other children, and peered through their legs. The three aggies rolled, and settled. The bluey came to rest within eighteen inches of the hole; it was the nearest. That meant the owner of the bluey would play first.

He crouched beside the furthest-away marble, a light green one with a red spiral in it called a twisty. If he could shoot this one into the hole, he could try for the next-furthest, and then finally the nearest, his own. But the other two boys had been cunning. They had deliberately let him get his bluey the nearest, and thrown theirs short. He hadn't a hope of getting the twisty in; he shot hard -- it left the ground and leapt past the hole. He straightened up with a grim face.

The second boy shot his own marble. It was a 'bird's-egg', a china marble with gold speckles on it. Ronnie envied this one the least, since what use was a marble if you couldn't see the light through it? But the gold flecks made it special. The boy took a long time over his shot, measuring the distance with his eyes, and swinging his bent finger back and forth like a golf-club. Ronnie held his breath. He wanted the bluey-boy to win. The others had so many, and the bluey-boy only the two beauties.

The shot came at last, and Ronnie was sure it was going in – it rolled along the uneven ground, bumping over the small half-submerged pebbles, its gold flakes glittering bravely – right to the brink of the hole. But it was a tricky hole. It had a rim, almost invisible but still enough to stop an aggie whose force was nearly spent. The bird's-egg was halted by it, just when it was about to drop in. The shooter let out a groan and Ronnie gave a sigh of relief.

The third boy stepped forward with a careless swagger. The twisty (now about a foot on the far side of the hole) was his best marble; he was playing it only to show off, and because he felt confident that he could win both the bird's-egg and the bluey, for he had plenty of other beauties he could have used. His strategy had worked so far; he had aimed to shoot last, reckoning that the other two, less experienced players, would both muff their shots and leave the field in good order for him to scoop all three aggies. So it seemed it would be, for his twisty was less than a foot on the far side of the hole where it had been overshot by the bluey-boy: the bird's-egg quivered on the very brink, where the most careless flick would tip it home; and the coveted bluey itself was still where it had first fallen, by no means too far for an expert like him to shoot it in. After he had done this, it would be child's play to win the others.

There was only one problem, and even Ronnie, with his incomplete knowledge of the game, could see what it was. The bird's-egg was in a direct line with the bluey that had to be shot first. They were playing according to the rule which says that if you touch one aggie with another, the next player collects any aggies you get into the hole. This meant that if the expert hit the bird's-egg in with the bluey, and if the bluey itself went in after it, then the bluey's owner would get them both, and the next turn as well.

There was only one way out. The expert had to shoot the bluey in a curve, avoiding the bird's-egg. This is possibly the most difficult shot there is, because even the breath of a passing aggie might shiver the bird's-egg in, and then who was to say whether they had actually touched or not? The expert hesitated, and then tried tactics.

'Knockers keepers,' he said as he crouched down.

He said it in a very casual tone, as if merely confirming what everybody knew. But there was an instant outcry from the other players, and from the crowd who had been playing earlier.

'Nuts to that! We haven't been playing knockers keepers all day!'

'Well, we are now.'

'We are not!'

'We are so. Every game is separate. Nobody called knockers losers for this game.'

'You don't have to call for each game! If nobody calls something different, it's same as the last game.'

'Well, I just did call something different.'

But he was howled down. He gave in fairly gracefully, having hardly expected to get away with his ploy. He shrugged his shoulders.

'Okay, okay. I don't care. I can still do it.'

A deep hush fell, and Ronnie, hardly aware of what he was doing, edged into the front line with the others to see better. The third player crouched down, his gangling knees up to his ears. His dirt-grained finger crooked behind the bluey. Ronnie saw its owner clutch the sides of his jacket in an agony of suspense.

The bluey moved off in a slow, deliberate curve. It was a beautiful shot, and it had to be. There wasn't a sound from the crowd as it rolled, as if under its own power, round in a wide arc, missing the poised bird's-egg and dropping nearly into the little earth cavity.

It lay there like a blue eye looking out of the ground.

A sound half-way between a sigh and a moan went round the circle. Ronnie couldn't look at the other boy. He stared at that unwinking lost eye.

Its new owner leapt up gleefully and pocketed it. He was so pleased with himself that he didn't even crouch for the next shot, but simply bent over from the waist and flicked the twisty towards the hole with a limp swing of his arm from the elbow. The chatter which had started among the children in response to his previous clever shot died on the instant; the twisty spun unerringly across the intervening space, in down one side of the hole, up the other, and then fell back into place – bringing the bird's-egg on top of it with a little final click.

Nobody spoke. Now Ronnie could look at the other boy. His hands were slowly relaxing on the edge of his jacket. He glanced uncertainly from face to face, not quite able to believe his luck. The third boy gave him a not unfriendly push from behind, and he stumbled forward and clumsily picked up the two aggies nestling together in the hole.

'I guess that's one way to win,' said the loser disgustedly.

'Sore loser!' taunted the crowd.

'Okay! Now you got three beauties. So play me again. Play your goldie!'

'No!'

'No fair to quit when you're winning.'

The bluey-boy scuffed his sneakers on the hard ground. He made a decision.

'Okay then. I'll play my goldie if you'll play my bluey!'

The richer boy tossed the bluey into the air and caught it again several times. It glittered like a precious sapphire in the thin sunlight.

'Want it back, huh? Think you can beat me? You only got those two through my bad luck.'

'You want to play, or don't you?'

'Sure!'

'Twosies!' suddenly said the other boy, the one who had lost the bird's-egg.

Ronnie was so caught up in the game by now that he forgot his shyness.

'What's "twosies"?' he asked the boy standing next to him.

'Don't you know? It means everyone throws two aggies.'

Though he had never been to school or been taught arithmetic, Ronnie saw at once that this meant twice as many aggies – six instead of three – and twice as much excitement. He could not help jumping up and down once, but he quickly took hold of himself.

The three players were once more poised on the throwing-line. Ronnie saw that his favourite player was having trouble deciding which aggie to hold on to, which two to play. Eventually he settled on the goldie and the twisty, retaining the bird's-egg.

The other two were not obliged to risk two beauties each, so they played one beauty and one ordinary aggie. The bird's-egg boy, smarting from its loss, carefully selected his least treasured beauty, a fairly common cat's-eye in good condition, which, Ronnie thought, only just counted as a beauty at all.

The signal was given, and the six aggies flashed, landed, rolled. The ground seemed covered with them. Ronnie gripped his hand hard round his own precious solitary aggie, like a talisman. As the bluey-boy moved to take the first shot, he caught Ronnie's eye. Ronnie swallowed. He gave a little nod of his head, a stiff little movement, with which he wanted to convey encouragement and support. The bluey-boy's face lost its grim look for a moment and he almost smiled.

The game moved quickly. The rich boy, as Ronnie thought of him, the riches being measured in aggies though he was the poorest-dressed, collared three aggies with his first turn, but two of them were the ordinary ones and the third the twisty which had been his to begin with. Still on the ground were the cat's-eye, the bluey – and the goldie, upon which every eye was hungrily fixed. They were all grouped near the hole, and it seemed certain that the other boy, whose turn it was, would get them all in one by one.

Ronnie was so keyed up he felt he couldn't bear to watch the ground. The aggies seemed to be dancing, he had concentrated on them for so long. So he decided to watch the bluey-boy's face instead, and guess from that what was happening.

It was not difficult, for a grim face can always grow three degrees grimmer, and that is what happened. His mouth tightened, drew down at the corners – one aggie gone. Ronnie was dying to see which, but even though he cheated with himself and glanced down, all he could see was the player's back as he scrabbled like a crab into position for the next shot. The face he was watching changed again to an expression of agonized expectation, teeth bared, brows frowning. Was this the goldie? The shot was taken in perfect silence; there was a gasp – then a sigh, and every head turned to look at the boy who was now immeasurably poorer than he had been a moment before.

Ronnie didn't have to look down to know that the goldie had passed to a new possessor. He lowered his eyes to his own sneakers. He knew the loser of this treasure must cry, who could help it? – and he didn't want to watch that.

The final aggie, not that it mattered now, followed the goldie into the already bulging bag of the bird's-egg boy.

The crowd began to break up.

'You want to play your last aggie?'

With lowered face, the boy shook his head. He was desperate enough however to try something. Ronnie saw him approach the third boy.

'Trade you.'

'What?'

'Your bird's-egg for my goldie.'

'You're nuts.'

Everyone had moved away now. The two winners were crouching together, gloating over their spoils; their aggies, tipped out of the bags, lay in carefully separated piles. Ronnie still stood there, fascinated, unable to move away from the scene of the battle, the sight of so much wealth.

Suddenly one of them noticed him.

'Say, kid,' he said, 'you got any aggies?'

'One.'

'You wanna play?'

Ronnie shook his head.

'Let's see what kind you got.'

Ronnie hesitated. Burnt into his memory was an incident he had once witnessed. A boy, smaller and even more timid than himself, had been persuaded into showing some bigger boys a toy from his pocket. A swift blow on his wrist had knocked the toy to the ground, whence it had been snatched up and made off with, its rightful owner left in the middle of the street howling with helpless outrage.

He looked from one boy to the other.

'You gonna grab it off me if I show you?'

'Naw! Why should we? We only wanna look. Is it a beauty?'

Slowly Ronnie drew his hand from his pocket, and held it before him. He uncurled the protective fingers a little, to show the aggie nestling in his palm. Its smooth, unplayed surface was misted with the heat of his hand, but the boys could see it was a rare treasure indeed – smaller than the usual size, and of a beautiful, glowing red.

'A peewee ruby!' breathed one. 'Boy!'

'It's a beauty all right!' agreed the other. 'Where'd you get it?'

'Found it,' said Ronnie, returning it to his pocket.

'Let's see it again.'

This time Ronnie dared to open his hand all the way. The peewee ruby glowed in his palm like fire and blood.

'Trade you.'

'What for?'

The boy moved to his pile and quickly selected his three best marbles, including the new-won goldie, and pocketed them.

'Any one of these others.'

'Naw.'

'Okay then. Any two.'

Ronnie felt a surge of delight pass over him. It was his first taste of power. At his feet lay riches, and the pleasures of free choice. But he looked again at his own aggie. No. It had been precious enough before, but since he had learnt its name and that it was coveted, its value had trebled.

'Naw.'

The boy debated with himself. 'Tell you what then. I'll lend you one to play with. If you win, you can keep it and I'll give you two others, any two you choose except my three beauties. If I win, you gotta give me your peewee.'

Ronnie was on the point of shaking his head again when he saw the other boy – the one who had lost all, or nearly all, his aggies – standing at some distance, watching them.

'I can't play. I never played.'

The two big boys looked at each other in comic astonishment.

'Where've ya bin? Ya musta bin drug up in a barn!'

Ronnie, who was unfamiliar with this taunt, said nothing. To him a barn held no insulting connotations, it was a fact of the landscape.

The bird's-egg boy spoke up again. His greed for the peewee ruby would not allow him to let Ronnie go.

'Okay, listen. I'll go easy on you. Tell you what. I'll play with my left hand. Waddaya say? Ain't that fair?'

Ronnie, who didn't know his left from his right, stood stock still, looking at the other boy in confusion.

'Okay?' he pressed.

'I dunno.'

'Aw, c'mon,' said the third boy. 'He don't wanna. Let him alone.'

The bird's-egg boy ignored him. 'What *would* you play for?' he persisted.

Ronnie muttered something.

'Whatcha say?'

'The goldie.'

'The *goldie?* Aw, heck . . .'

The third boy nudged him hard. 'Go ahead. You can't lose, can you? He's just a baby. He ain't never even played.' He had scented an exciting contest.

'Okay. Your peewee against my goldie!'

Ronnie's throat closed up with horror and his heart threatened to thud out of his chest and away down the road by itself. He put a hand up to his breastbone as if to hold it in, and his peewee fell and rolled on the ground. Instantly he snatched it up. He wanted to cry. He thought he was going to. What had he done? The aggie he loved was as good as lost.

The crowd of children had magically reassembled, as if, scattered about the street and vacant lot, they had sensed the onset of a new match. The bluey-boy stood aside, as Ronnie had at first.

Now it was Ronnie's grubby sneaker-toe on the line, newly defined in the grit with a sharp stick. Standing side by side with his opponent, he felt his essential inferiority to this tough, worldly-wise, practised towny boy. Older than Ronnie, two inches taller, his hair untouched by a brush, his legs filthy, he was everything Ronnie was not and longed to be. And soon he would own Ronnie's aggie, and thus would have everything in the world that mattered.

'Okay, let's call the rules,' he said competently. 'Ya wanna call something?'

Ronnie looked at him mutely.

'Knockers takers or knockers losers?'

'I dunno.'

'Knockers takers,' he said. 'Ya want inners winners?'

'What is it?'

The older boy rolled his eyes up for the benefit of the audience.

'You don't know nothin', do ya? It's if you get your aggie straight in with your first throw, you collect both aggies and the game's over.'

Ronnie looked at the hole. It was so far away – impossible to dream he could throw it in or anywhere near in.

'G'wan,' urged his opponent craftily. 'The peewee's smaller, it'll roll in easier.' The opposite was in fact the truth, as he knew. Smaller, lighter aggies were the hardest to win with. When he himself had got possession of the peewee he would keep it as a trophy, never play it. Among sophisticated players, peewees were never played against regular aggies, only in special peewee matches.

'Okay then,' said Ronnie hopelessly. What difference could it make?

'On your mark. Get set. Throw!'

Ronnie didn't even know how to do that properly. He instinctively felt that the regulation underarm throw would not bring the aggie anywhere near the mark. So he raised his arm over his shoulder and tossed the ruby, with a feeling of angry desperation, in the general direction of the hole.

The crowd broke into laughter as the peewee performed a series of bounces, overtaking the goldie which was rolling decorously down the straight in the approved fashion.

Ronnie hated the laughter. He watched the peewee bouncing and knew it must be getting scratched; he felt each impact on his own flesh. He had thrown his treasure away, and for what? Because another boy had looked sad? Because he wanted the goldie for himself? He couldn't understand. A moment ago the ruby had been part of his pocket, part of his hand, part of his existence. Now it had disappeared somewhere down there in a blur of tears and he would never touch it again.

But something was wrong. The laughter had stopped on a sudden jarring note, and everyone was bent forward, peering.

'Geez!' came an awe-stricken whisper. 'It's in!'

'The kid got it right in!'

'It's inners winners – he's won 'em both, first throw!'

Ronnie brushed his tears away with a hand still innocent of contact with the gritty ground. He looked incredulously at the hole. His little red aggie winked at him from smack in the middle of it. The goldie lay a good foot away, catching the sun like a solid gold pearl.

Someone gave him a shove.

'Go get 'em, kiddo. They're yours!'

The other boy was justifiably dumbfounded and furious.

'No fair – ' he began, but was drowned out by hoots and jeers. The crowd, who had recently tasted the bitterness of defeat and beggary at the hands of this marble-millionaire, was delighted at the chance to turn on him in his discomfiture.

'Shut up, sore loser! It was *you* called inners winners!'

'He'd a beat you anyhow! He's a genius!'

Several hands banged Ronnie on the back as he walked unsteadily to the hole. He bent down. As his hands touched, simultaneously, the peewee and the goldie, as he lifted them and held them side by side to the light, he felt a queer sensation. It was, in actual fact, his first experience of tangible, definite, positive happiness. It was so strong it was possible to confuse it with pain, and he felt he might cry again.

The boy he had been playing with was muttering something about beginners' luck, but Ronnie didn't hear. He started to walk away, oblivious of everything except that he held a beautiful aggie in each hand. Something gripped his arm.

'Ya wanna play again? Twosies?'

Ronnie shook free. 'Naw!' he said.

'Aw, c'mon! No fair to quit when you're –'

But Ronnie was already running, running back round the corner of the store where his father's truck was parked. He scrambled inside the cabin which felt like a haven. He could not but suppose they would come after him like a pack of hounds to drag him back and force him to yield up his miraculously won prizes. But safely in the cabin, high off the ground and surrounded by solid steel and glass, he felt secure.

He laid a hand on each knee, opened the fingers slowly, and gazed. Relief and happiness poured over him, he sank into it and it engulfed him as solidly as a billion grains of wheat when you jump into a heap of them, and work yourself down till you are buried to the neck.

Suddenly someone tapped on the glass by his head. He started with fright and thrust the aggies back into his pockets.

It was the bluey-boy. He had climbed up on the outside of the truck and was hanging on by the door-handle, his face level with Ronnie's.

Ronnie rolled down the window.

'Whatcha want?'

The boy looked at him dumbly for a moment.

'Willya trade?' he croaked at last.

'What for?'

'My – the goldie for the bird's-egg.'

'Naw!' cried Ronnie instantly, adding, like the bigger boys, 'Are you nuts?'

The other boy's lips trembled.

'I had it years already,' he said. 'It was always my best beauty.'

'So whyja play it then?'

'Whyja play yours?'

Ronnie was silenced. He did not understand to this moment what had possessed him to risk losing his aggie.

'Something gets hold of ya,' muttered the other boy.

Neither of them spoke for a while. The boy changed hands and hung on to the handle precariously.

'What's your name?' asked Ronnie.

'Gordie,' said the other. He gave his nose a quick wipe on his sleeve, bending his head down to his arm to do it. 'You won't trade me, then?'

'I dunno.'

'What's yours?'

'Ronnie.'

'Whereja live?'

'That way,' said Ronnie, pointing east. 'A hundred miles.'

'Geez! On a farm?'

'Yeah.'

There was another pause.

'You won't trade, then?'

'Dja go to school?'

'Sure,' said Gordie, looking surprised. 'Don't you?'

'I live too far.'

'Geez, you lucky stiff!'

Ronnie was so astounded by this remark that the goldie fell from his hand and almost got lost down the gear-shaft. He scrambled for it frantically and recovered it. The other boy hung through the window and watched with held breath.

'You better trade. You'll only lose it.'

'But I want to keep it.'

'You'll lose it, sure. On a farm . . . it'll drop in the muck or a cow'll eat it.'

'We ain't got *cows!*' said Ronnie with a sudden snort of laughter.

'What have you got then?'

'Just wheat. And some hens.'

'They lay eggs?'

'Sure! Whatcha think we keep 'em for?'

'I dunno. Dja ever see a hen lay an egg?'

'Sure, millions of times.'

'I mean . . . You seen it comin' out?'

'Sure.'

'Sure must look funny.' The boy turned red, put his head down against the window-sill, and choked with laughter. Ronnie was puzzled and said nothing.

'Ronnie!'

Ronnie turned his head sharply at the sound of his father's peremptory call. Gordie lost his hold and fell backwards down the side of the truck. Hanging out of the window, Ronnie saw him spreadeagled in the mud. But he wasn't hurt. They caught each other's eyes and simultaneously burst out laughing.

Ronnie saw his father in the doorway of the store, a big box in his arms.

'Come and help your mother.'

He opened the door promptly and scrambled down backwards, jumping from the last stepping-place. Half on purpose, he tripped, and sat down in the mud beside Gordie. They were laughing so hysterically by now that neither of them could get up. Ronnie could feel the wet soaking through the seat of his trousers. It felt glorious – the cold, wicked touch of independence and freedom.

Then he felt something else – his father's big hand under his arm, hiking him to his feet.

'Get up from there! What do you think you're doing?'

'I fell, Pa!'

'You'll be in dutch when your mother sees the mess you're in. Get in the store now, and help her with the stuff.'

He ignored Gordie, still sprawling. Gordie was no concern of his.

With a pang of unease which was almost, but not quite, fear, Ronnie dashed into the store. His mother was there, helping the storeman to pack the last of the supplies into a box. He stopped still in the doorway and looked at her as if for the first time. Letting himself fall in the mud had, for the moment, put a distance between him and her; he noticed for the first time that her smooth, bunned hair was a little grey, that her face was rougher-looking and had much less colour in it than town women's. He noticed her clothes, the old, plain, faded dress which he had known since before he knew anything, longer now than other women's skirts, and different in other ways that he couldn't analyse. It hung down below her coat, which was relatively new, but still not pretty, only sensible and dark and warm. He looked at her whole figure and noticed it, too, was not like other women's, being big-boned, too tall, a little stooped. Ronnie stood open-mouthed with dismay, in the clarity of that moment of independent perception.

But it passed. She turned, and smiled at him, and it passed on the instant into the intimacy, almost one-ness, wherein she was, always had been and always would be so much a part of him that he didn't see her, any more than he saw his own nose.

'Here, take this box for me, will you, Ronnie?'

She pointed to a small box and he ran to pick it up. As he bent down he heard her gasp.

'Good grief, what've you been doing to yourself?'

'I fell, Mother.'

He dreaded her disapproval. He turned his face up and threw her a look of appeal. You never knew with her. She might be angry – every dirty garment had to be washed painfully by hand with a washboard and mangle, and drying was a problem in this damp season – or she might let it go, either out of a flash of good nature and understanding, or just from sheer tiredness. Ronnie was lucky this time. Her rather grim face softened.

'Oh well . . . you're not often careless.'

He was deeply relieved. It was especially important to him that she shouldn't spoil today by scolding him. To thank her, he pressed his head against the warmth of her coat for a moment, then picked up the box and ran staggering with it to the door.

'Now don't go running with that, or you'll trip again.'

He slowed down and carried the box to the truck with conscientious slowness. As soon as his father had relieved him of it, and of his duty, he immediately looked round for Gordie. He couldn't see him, and his heart sank. He felt a strong sense of loss, and instinctively put his hands in his pockets to make sure the aggies were still there. They were. It was something more – even more – important that had gone.

But it hadn't, for as he and his mother and father settled themselves up in the high cabin of the truck, with him on the outside so he could fly his hand out of the window and feel the wind snatching at it on the way home, he caught sight of Gordie peeping round the edge of the store building. A great joy made a swelling inside his chest. He forgot himself completely and screamed, just as his father was switching on the engine:

'Gordie! C'm'ere!'

His mother looked round sharply – she seldom heard him yell, even with pain. Ronnie was beckoning wildly. The other boy, emboldened, ran to the side of the truck and hoisted himself up again.

'Here!'

Gordie held out his hand instantly, his face alive with happiness. Ronnie dropped the goldie into it. In another moment, the bird's-egg, with its glinting gold fragments, had been passed to him. The truck was just beginning to move.

Gordie dropped off backwards, landing this time on his feet.

'Say, thanks a million!'

Ronnie waved and leant out of the window so far that his mother had to catch hold of the seat of his pants.

'See you in thirty days from now!' he yelled at the top of his lungs as the truck roared away from the curb.

'Sure! See ya!'

Ronnie waved till Gordie was out of sight. Then he sank back into his narrow place. He heard, as if from far away, his mother warning him that he'd fall out and be killed if he kept leaning out of windows that way. After a while his father, with his eyes on the beginning of the long, straight road that would lead them home, asked:

'Who was that, anyway?'

'My friend,' answered Ronnie, looking at the horizon.

The Samaritans and Young People
ANTHONY LAWTON

Who are the Samaritans? What do they do? Who should call them? This explanation shows that Samaritans are ordinary people who do nothing spectacular, but they are always there, and it is all right for anyone to call at any time for any reason.

MONICA DICKENS

*

What is a friend? This is what a fourteen-year-old girl said a friend was: 'A friend don't talk behind your back. If they are a true friend they help you get out of trouble and they will always be right behind you and they will help you through stuff.' That's what the Samaritans do – they befriend people when they are in trouble.

Not all of us have friends we can talk to when we are troubled, and sometimes the friends and relations we *could* talk to are not there when we need them. There are occasions when you want to talk about something too personal to tell friends or family and want to be sure no one knows what you are doing. You may even want to talk *about* your friends or family! The Samaritans offer someone who will act like a friend to whom you can talk at any time of the day or night at each of the 160 centres in Britain and Ireland. The most important aspect of this is listening to whatever the caller wants to talk about, and *helping* the caller to talk about how they feel, what is going wrong, and what can be done. Sometimes just talking things out is enough. At other times decisions may have to be made. Although the Samaritans are 'right behind you' they never tell you what to do; they try to help you calm down and decide for yourself. This is not always achieved in one meeting or one telephone conversation; it may be over weeks or even months of contact.

The girl said that a friend 'don't talk behind your back'. For that reason everything told to the Samaritans is totally confidential; nothing is said to parents or friends, to husbands or wives or lovers, to the police, to doctors or social workers; nothing to anybody unless the caller wants something said. This is why so many people feel it is safe to tell the Samaritans very personal things and this feeling of safety is increased for some people because they do not even have to give a name. Other people prefer to give at least a christian name, and some prefer a face-to-face meeting, although it is with a total stranger, because it is easier to talk to a stranger than to someone you know.

It doesn't matter how old, or young, you are, or what you are calling about, the Samaritans never try and persuade you to do anything. They believe that the best way to help someone is to help him sort things out for himself, and whatever his age he can be responsible if he is allowed to be so. After all, the person who knows best how he feels is the person in trouble.

Young people often believe that the Samaritans is only for adults. They probably think it is only for people who are really desperate and suicidal, but this is not the case. Something that does not seem so bad at the moment may quickly become worse if bottled up, and the Samaritans are there – a friendly ear at the end of a phone. Nowadays teenagers and people even younger than that are telephoning or visiting us more and more often. Suicide attempts are increasing amongst young people, more than in any other age group. We know young people have as many difficulties and pressures to face as their elders, many of whom seem to have forgotten how difficult life can be and fail to take time to listen.

Many different problems are brought to the Samaritans – a

love-affair or marriage is going badly or breaking up; someone important to you dies; you are feeling increasingly lonely
– and such problems may be aggravated by lack of money,
lack of housing or unemployment. There are particular
difficulties about being young ... learning about oneself, becoming independent, finding friends, discovering about sex
and sexuality, coping at school, problems with home and
parents, loneliness and boredom, when everyone says your
youth ought to be the happiest time of your life! It is often
difficult to find someone who will listen, someone who re-
alizes that what may seem trivial in the light of experience is
extremely serious to the person actually experiencing it. You
need someone who does not answer every problem with
'You'll grow out of it'. It is a sad fact that in Britain alone
three people under the age of sixteen kill themselves every
month. Those three young people never grow old enough to
grow out of it.

Young people's feelings go up and down very quickly.
These feelings can be very intense and young people, often
lacking the words to describe them, use actions instead. They
may run away from home or school or become involved in
petty crime. They may suffer in silence with a growing inner
loneliness. As a last resort some will attempt suicide. Many
people who do this do not really want to die, they just don't
want to go on living with things as they are. Sometimes they
are saying, 'I've had enough ... help me;' other times, 'I've
had enough and it's your fault ... you'll be sorry;' or it can be
an attempt to find some temporary peace. Nearly always a
warning of some sort is given but possibly not noticed. But,
however bad someone is feeling, whatever the reason, the
Samaritans are always available. It is not dangerous for people
to talk to each other about their problems, even to the extent
of talking about suicide. The person who shares his troubles
is more likely to be helped than harmed. The service is manned
by volunteers who work in their spare time. These volunteers,

like the callers, are all ages and come from all backgrounds. They are carefully chosen and trained to be good listeners: no formal qualifications are needed, and despite the name it is not a religious organization.

Indeed, the whole idea of the Samaritans is based on the belief that talking about troubles is helpful. In this way, as the girl said of a friend, 'they help you get out of trouble and they will always be right behind you and they will help you through stuff.' One of the Samaritans' leaflets says:

'When you are having a bad time, it may help to talk to someone you trust . . . parent, friend, teacher, counsellor, social worker, priest . . .

'If you can't find someone you trust, or you don't want to tell them . . . try the SAMARITANS.'

Remember
Ring/write/visit Samaritans any time.
No one need know.

KILL-A-LOUSE WEEK AND OTHER STORIES

Susan Gregory

The new head arrives at Davenport Secondary just at the beginning of the 'Kill-a-Louse' campaign. Soon the whole school is in uproar . . .

YATESY'S RAP

Jon Blake

It was Ol's idea to play the Christmas concert. His second idea was to get a band together. A most unlikely band it turned out to be. Half of them couldn't play, most of them didn't like each other, and none of them had ever been on a stage. And then Yatesy arrived, with his reputation for being kicked out of several schools for fighting.

BREAKING GLASS

Brian Morse

When the Red Army drops its germ bomb on Leicester, the affected zone is sealed off permanently – with Darren and his sister Sally inside it. Immune to the disease which kills Sally, Darren must face alone the incomprehensible hatred of two of the few survivors trapped with him. And the haunting question is: why did Dad betray them?

UNEASY MONEY
Robin F. Brancato

What would *you* do if you won a fortune? That's what happens when Mike Bronti buys a New Jersey lottery ticket to celebrate his eighteenth birthday. Suddenly, everything looks possible: gifts for his family, treats for his friends, a new car for himself – but things don't work out quite as Mike expects them to. A funny, sensitive story about everyone's favourite fantasy.

THE TRICKSTERS
Margaret Mahy

The Hamiltons gather at their holiday house for their customary celebration of midsummer Christmas in New Zealand, but it is to be a Christmas they'll never forget. For the warm, chaotic family atmosphere is chilled by the unexpected arrival of three sinister brothers – the Tricksters.

THREE'S A CROWD
Jennifer Cole

How much fun can you have when your parents are away? No housework, no homework, a BIG party, and plenty of boys. Hey, who's throwing pizza around and where's Mollie disappeared to with that strange guy? (The first book in the *Sisters* trilogy).

LOCKED IN TIME
Lois Duncan

When seventeen-year-old Nore Robbins arrives at the old Louisiana plantation home of her father and his new wife, she is prepared for unhappiness. Although Lisette, her new mother, is exotically beautiful, Nore senses evil, and why is her son Gabe so bitter about life? As time passes she pieces together a strange and terrible truth about the family. She alone is a threat to their secret – and threats must be destroyed.

MOVING IN
June Oldham

Sparky sixth-former Ellen thinks it's about time she made a bid for independence. She can cope with the eccentric landlord of the unfurnished room in a terraced house, and with her school's obsession with her moral welfare, but the two young men who appear on the scene are the real problem.

CAN'T STOP US NOW
Fran Lantz

Reg Barthwaite, pop promoter and manager, knows he's on to a winner when he picks C.C., Robin, Gail and Annette to form a new rock band. With their talent and his connections he's sure he's got the latest pop sensation on his hands. But the girls discover that making it in the music business isn't that easy, and as Reg becomes ever more insistent that they play on his terms, they are forced to question just what they want – fame at any price?